D1239427

Follow Your Star

Follow Your Star

Compiled by Ruth H. Wagner
Designed by Bradbury Thompson

Published by
The C.R. Gibson Company
Norwalk, Connecticut

Printed in the United States of America
Library of Congress Catalog Card Number: 69-14274
SBN 8378-1855-9

Contents

These Stars...

I

These stars will wait until we come again.
We need not fear. Their steadfastness is proof
Against the vagrancy of altered need
That sends us homeward now, to seek a roof
Where fire awaits our coming.
In its glow,
I shall scrawl out a letter to a friend;
Your turning pages will count off the hours
That have no other voice...
And then, day's end:
I shall put by my pen, and you your book;
We shall bank up the coals, and climb the stairs,
Content to leave to the soft-fingered dark
Our shadowy-cornered room, our empty chairs.

Tomorrow, we shall think and speak our thoughts...
We shall touch hands... and do each little chore:
The cooking of our food... our garden's care...
The brushing by of leaves before the door.
We shall make laughter out of bafflement...
And meet the wind... and watch the day's declining...

Then we shall stand again beneath these stars,
To feel how certain is their nightly shining.

Bonaro Overstreet

Chapter One

Hold the Present Close

Chapter One

Be glad of life because it gives you
the chance to love and to work and to play
and to look up at the stars.

Henry Van Dyke

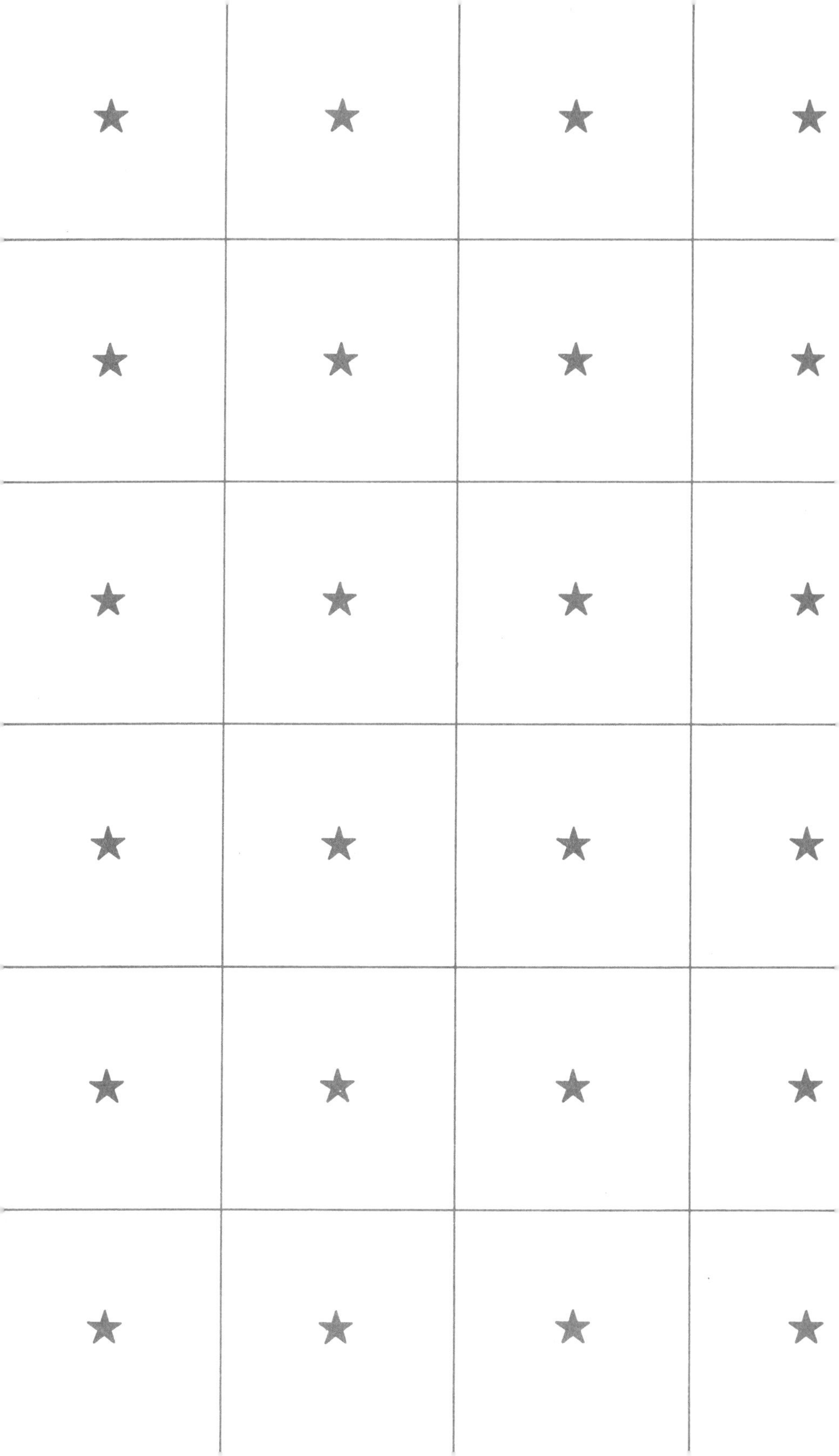

3

For a Bride and Groom

I wish you many days of gentle weather
With sun to spare.
I wish you violent storms to face together,
Conquests to share.

As much as quiet days, as much as all
Remembered sun,
Marriage needs struggles that two hearts recall
That two have won.

Jane Merchant

4

Grief can take care of itself,
but to get the full value of joy
you must have somebody
to divide it with.

Mark Twain

5

Happiness sneaks in through a door
you didn't know you left open.

John Barrymore

6

Happiness grows at our own firesides,
and is not to be picked in strangers' gardens.

Douglas Jerrold

The Prophet

7

Your children are not your children.
They are the sons and daughters of
  Life's longing for itself.
They come through you but not from you,
And though they are with you
  yet they belong not to you.
You may give them your love
  but not your thoughts,
For they have their own thoughts.
You may house their bodies
  but not their souls,
For their souls dwell in the house of tomorrow,
  which you cannot visit, not even in your dreams.
You may strive to be like them,
  but seek not to make them like you.
For life goes not backward nor tarries
  with yesterday.

Kahlil Gibran

8

When one becomes a father, then first one becomes a son. Standing by the crib of one's own baby, with that world-old pang of compassion and protectiveness toward this so little creature that has all its course to run, the heart flies back in yearning and gratitude to those who felt just so toward one's self. Then for the first time one understands the homely succession of sacrifices and pains by which life is transmitted and fostered down the stumbling generations of men.

Christopher Morley

A Mother's Prayer

Dear Lord, Please help me understand
my four boys, not including my husband.

Dear Lord, That means five adolescents,
including my husband.

Dear Lord, Please help me teach my sons
how to stand on their own two feet, and
at the same time not step on
somebody else's toes, and
Help me appease four different kinds of
appetite at each meal, and
Help me find a ready cure for acne, so
that everybody in the house can eat
chocolate cake the same year, and
Help me serve a main course at dinner
my sons have *not* had at school
for lunch that day, and
Help my husband give them a smack,
when it's called for, instead of an
increase in allowance.

Dear Lord, Please help me not to hear so
much, see so much, and say so much, and
Help me not to correct so much, and
Help somebody invent a hi-fi that will
play so loud and no louder, and
Help my boys talk about something
besides Baseball, because I *can't* have
Tallulah Bankhead to dinner
with them every night, and
Help find a way for them to learn their
piano lessons in only ten minutes
of practice a day, and

Help me, once in a while, have my hair
cut instead of pulling it, and
Help hand-me-downs fit somebody after
being in the closet three years.

Dear Lord, Please help me explain to
Jeff that he does *not* have to approve of
the girls Warren and George take out, and
Help me remember to buy name tapes, and
Help me have the patience to sew
them on, and
Help me talk softly and carry
a big layer cake, and
Help me find a dessert that is not bad
for weight, skin, and teeth, and that all
my sons will like the same night, and
Help me find a dress that all my
five men *and* I will like.

Dear Lord, Please make Geometry
go away, and
Please help me understand Space, even
if there is none in my closets, and
Help my boys find girls, someday, who
are good enough for them, even though
I won't think so at the time, and
Help Fordham Law School teach George
as much about Blackstone as he now
knows about Spink's *Baseball Guide*, and
Help Columbia University teach
Warren there is something else in the
world besides the Theater and Music, and
Help Jeffrey believe that giving up
catsup, at least for breakfast,
will improve his chances for
becoming a bullfighter, and
Help Douglas, at 12, feel like 16. Me, too.

Dear Lord, Please help me decide when
I'm to stop behaving like a sergeant and
start acting like a mother, and
Help me decide what to do with all
those sneakers, ranging from size 6 to
size 11½, plus a left 5½, and
Help me win one checker game, even
against our youngest son, and
Help manufacturers of black socks sew
an initial into them so my five males
don't all yell at once, "That pair's mine," and
Help me to know what to wear and what
not to wear, when one son says it makes
me look like Marilyn Monroe and another
says it makes me look like Marjorie Main—
while the noncommittal two
continue to buck for allowance increases.

Dear Lord, Please accept my thanks for
giving my boys a sense of humor
if it is often at my expense, which is
too expensive, and
Thank you for George's liking Wall
Street quotations and not the drums, and
Thank you for Warren's liking the piano
and not the drums, and
Thank you for Jeffrey's liking the guitar
and not the drums, and
Thank you for Douglas' liking science
and not the drums.

Dear Lord, Thank you, thank you,
thank you for my husband and
for giving us four sons.
Dear Lord.

Sylvia R. Lyons

The Seeker

10

One may reject a Savior
In independent pride.
One may rebel against a King.
A Lord may be denied.

But God is very subtle,
Evade Him as we may.
God knows that it is difficult
To turn a Child away.

Jane Merchant

11

New father rushing from hospital:
"It's a father!
I'm a girl! I'm a girl!"

The American Weekly

Unexceptional Behavior

12

The children play quietly,
Coloring books,
Dressing their dolls,
Building new nooks,
Piecing out puzzles
And games of their own;
The children are angels—
Till I'm on the phone.

Jean Carpenter Mergard

Question and Answer

13

There was that story we had read in *The New Yorker*. My wife and I had cherished it over the years. It had seemed the perfect anticipation of parental problems which we knew were bound to come our way.

I have in mind the anecdote about the little girl who one day confronted her mother with the sixty-four-dollar question, "Mommy dear, where did I come from?" The mother inhaled deeply, blushed, and shut the door. Although the dreaded moment had overtaken her sooner than she expected, she realized that as a modern she must face the facts, and face them squarely. Accordingly, she swallowed her modesty and plunged into a long and detailed, if un-Darwinian, lecture on the origin of the species. With a mother's generosity she gave her all. Yet to her amazement she found that her daughter, instead of being fascinated by her account of life's sweet mystery, was becoming increasingly bored by it. Finally the mother could stand it no longer. "Why, dear," she demanded, "If you won't listen to my answers, did you ask me such a question?" "Oh, don't you see, Mommy," replied the daughter, "in school today Agnes said she came from Buffalo."

John Mason Brown

14

There ought to be an organization of
Parents Anonymous—P.A.'s—
those who have fought and won the battle
of saying "No!" and sticking to it.
Then when some parent finds himself slipping
he could call for reinforcements.

Marcelene Cox

15

When God wants an important thing done
in His world, or a wrong righted,
He goes about it in a roundabout fashion.
He never lets loose thunderbolts
nor stirs up earthquakes.
He simply has a tiny baby born.

Margaret Applegarth

The Secret

16

There is a secret part to me
That does amazing things:
It is an actress on TV,
A butterfly who sings,
The author of a winning play,
An artist planning sketches.
The rest of me keeps house all day
And, as expected, fetches
Lost dolls and balls, bakes hot cross buns,
Mends bruises like no other
For my adored, unknowing ones,
To whom I'm simply Mother!

Jean Carpenter Mergard

17

The most important thing
a father can do for his children
is to love their mother.

The Reverend Theodore Hesburgh

Necessary Evil

18

My stand is firm and resolute
   On letting children watch TV;
It's just a parent's substitute
   For his responsibility.

It undermines the family ties,
   Discounts ideals that should be taught.
It stoops the shoulders, strains the eyes,
   Disparages creative thought.

But halfway through the day I find
Without it I would lose my mind.

Janet Henry

19

If it isn't heart-keeping,
it isn't house-keeping.

Marcelene Cox

Sheltered Wife

20

He seldom brings home flowers
   or candy;
With honeyed phrases, he's not
   very handy.
You ask, "If he loves you, where
   is the proof?"
Well, he's up there now, fixing
   the roof.

Marie Dane

Table Manners for Children

21

The first point to be established is that one does not sit *on* the table. One sits on the chair, and in such a way that all four legs touch the floor at the same time. (I am of course speaking of the four legs of the chair; children only *seem* to have four legs.) For children who will rock and tilt anyway, I suggest [a] built-in benches, [b] the practice of instilling in such children a sense of *noblesse oblige*, so that when they go crashing back onto their heads they go bravely and gallantly and without pulling the tablecloth, the dinner and a full set of dishes with them. This latter may sound severe, but it will be excellent training if they should ever enter the marines, or even Schrafft's.

We don't have to bother about little niceties such as which fork is the shrimp fork (at these prices, who is giving them shrimp?). We shall suppose, and safely, that the child has only one fork. If this child is interested in good manners and/or the sanity of his parents he will not use the fork to [a] comb his hair, [b] punch holes in the tablecloth, or [c] remove buttons from his jacket. Nor will he ever, under any circumstances, place the tines of the fork under a full glass of milk and beat on the handle with a spoon.

So far as the food itself is concerned, it would be well for the child to adopt a philosophical attitude about that dreary procession of well-balanced meals by reminding himself that in eighteen years or less he will be free to have frozen pizza pies and fig bars every single night. And he should remember, too, that there is a right way and a wrong way to talk about broccoli. Instead of the gloomy mutter "Oh, broccoli again—ugh!" how much better the cheery "I guess I'll eat this broccoli first and get it over with."

Finally, children should be made to understand that no matter how repellent they find a given vegetable,

21

they may not stuff large handfuls of it into their pockets, particularly if the vegetable is creamed. This sorry but unfortunately common practice not only deprives the child of necessary vitamins but frequently exposes him to intemperate criticism and even physical violence.

Jean Kerr

Marginal Note on a Milk Bill

22

Oh, I could buy mink in the
latest fashion,
And other such luxuries,
If I could but learn to control
my passion
For foolish necessities!

Georgie Starbuck Galbraith

23

Teen-age girl on telephone:
"If that click on the extension is you, Mother,
remember that wire-tap evidence is inadmissable."

J.B. Handelsman

Dining Out

24

How nice to be able
To sit down to eat
Where all at the table
Can cut their own meat!

Janet Henry

Four

25

Four is too big for his breeches,
Knows infinitely more than his mother,
Four is a matinee idol
To Two-and-a-Half, his brother.
Four is a lyric composer,
Raconteur extraordinaire,
Four gets away with murder,
Out of line, and into hair.
Where Four is, there dirt is also,
And nails and lengths of twine,
Four is Mr. Fix-it
And all of his tools are mine.
Four barges into everything
(Hearts, too) without a knock.
Four will be five on the twelfth of July,
And I wish I could stop the clock.

Elsie Gibbs

It Could be Worse

26

A mother with a cookie jar
That empties fast (a week is par)
Feels sometimes, when her back is aching,
As if she's almost always baking.
Forever she must measure, mix,
And pour, and scrape the pan that sticks—
But think how sad she'd feel, how beaten,
To have her cookies go uneaten!

Richard Armour

23

Mother's Day

27 "Sometimes I wish they'd dispense with Mother's Day," the woman said to the teen-ager. "I know my children love me; I wish they didn't feel they have to go out and spend their money on cards and gifts.

"Then, too, as an adult I love my own mother dearly and enjoy doing things for her, but Mother's Day makes it an obligation. Not because she expects anything or would be hurt if it weren't forthcoming, but because the advertisers have made it almost a must."

The girl looked back with a kind of troubled astonishment. "Why, I suppose," she said, "I just never thought of it like that. I mean from a young person's point of view it's fun. I like buying my mother a gift—especially now that I'm earning my own money. This year I'm getting her a lovely slip and a corsage. I've been thinking about it all week, looking forward to getting paid so that I could."

And suddenly the event falls into new perspective. Why, of course, Mother's Day, like practically every other holiday—is for the children!

The dancing eyes, the secrets. The giggling, "Stay out of my room!"... The pot holders woven at school and hidden under a bed.... The kindergarten's crepe paper carnations.

And a small girl's sly, "Have you got some material I can use? I mean *big* material big enough for a big person to wear if somebody was going to make that person a dress?" And submitting to being measured around the waist and draped in an ancient rose print you've dug out of the attic. And warning, "Dear, it's pretty hard to make a dress. I mean you ought to be older and have a pattern."

And the blithe reply born out of the miracle of faith and love, "Oh, I don't need any pattern, I can see it in my mind just as plain—how pretty you'll look in this dress." Aghast at this revelation, she claps her hand over her mouth while you pretend not to have heard.

And a son's dragging you to the drugstore to "look around," while he slips proudly up to the cosmetic counter to spend a whole dollar on cologne.

No, there's no out for us. Even the people who originally thought up Mother's Day probably got a greater glow out of it than their mothers. Gazing at the heap of presents, nibbling burnt toast eagerly served in bed, many a mother will secretly agree, "It is more blessed to give than to receive."

But her heart will be full, nonetheless. For she in her own way knows the pleasure of giving pleasure—by simply being the object and center of all this.

This is her secret on Mother's Day. This is the part she plays in the sweet conspiracy of love.

Marjorie Holmes

There's Something Nice About Having Them Around

28

Their children never wreck the place
Or make their weary parents race
To ascertain who "murdered" whom;
They never litter up a room,
Defy their elders, trample flowers,
Or break a windowpane—like ours.

And yet we'd rather have our own
For ours are youngsters... theirs are grown.

Ruth and Hal Chadwick

25

Christmas Grows on Many Trees

During the twelve weeks that I've taught elementary school youngsters, I've received many fringe benefits. These include all of the "wrong" statements found in essays that are twice as delightful as the right ones.

Last November and December, they came as thick as chalkdust. I read urgent news about Round John Virgin and the unfortunate shepherds who fell on their faces and were sore afterward.

Unlike their Christmas observations, most of the students' comments about Thanksgiving weren't really wrong—they were just expressed in that wonderfully original way of children. Here's what I mean:

"Thanksgiving is the day set aside for everybody to be happy. Oh. Except turkeys."

"One of the oldest of all Thanksgiving customs is to come on Thursday."

"The Pilgrims invited the Indians to their first Thanksgiving dinner. They did all sorts of nice things for the Indians whether they liked it or not. They were the first good Samericans."

On November 21, I received an eyewitness account of the landing at Plymouth Rock as reported by an enthusiastic little nine-year-old girl. Historically, I don't suppose her report is worth much—but as an example of unconscious humor, it's priceless:

"Wow! Look! There they finely come now! It looks like they are getting ready to land on Plymouth Rock. Yes, oh Yes, they *are!* They know that in these days it is not a chicken. It is a landing place. But look! Here come the Indians rolling their war hoops. Oh I cannot stand to look any more!"

It ends right there. After all, you can hardly be an eyewitness when you stop looking. I would like to thank three of her classmates, however, for furnishing

the information about what happened next:
"They came to America so they could have the right to have four fathers if they wanted to."
"One thing they learned from the Indians was how to smoke through a piece of pipe."
"The Indians finally grew to like the Pilgrims. The way they grew to like them was scalloped."

Youngsters usually have glowing comments about the Christmas season. But one little fellow didn't quite have the spirit last year when it came to the subject of mistletoe, e.g.: "Mistletoe means watch out for slobry girls."

His best friend concluded: "A good thing to remember about standing under mistletoe is don't."

Everyone has heard the story of Dickens' "A Christmas Carol," but here are some "facts" about that masterpiece that I never suspected:
"There is no such thing as a humbug but it is old and grouchy when there is."
"Everybody was taught how to act Christmasy by Tidt Tim."
"He taught them about the spirit that was started when the little Baby Jesus was born in Creche, a suburb of Bethlehem."

During that last month . . . , the Christmas spirit seemed willing but the thought processes were a little weak:

Question: Who were the Druids and where did they live? *Answer:* I don't remember, but whoever they are and wherever they live I wish them a merry Christmas.
"10 Xmases equal 1 Christmas."
"To celebrate Christmas in England, they sometimesdly chopped off the head of the biggest bore and carried it around on a platter."

Three very young poets had these charming observations about Christmas trees:

"A star is for living in heaven when it is not for wearing in a Christmas tree's hair."

"Pine trees give us Christmas and turpentine."

"Pine trees are not the only Christmas trees. Christmas grows on many kinds of trees."

You're probably familiar with the way very young children can inadvertently twist the words of songs into entirely different sentiments. Christmas carols are no exception.

Being responsible for the preparation of the Christmas program, I tried to teach Christmas carols to a group of first graders. The first time through, it sounded as though the entire class had changed "Round yon Virgin, Mother and Child" to "Onion version, Mother and Child."

They ended their "onion version" of "Silent Night" with these lyrics: "Sleep in half and in peace.... Sleep in half and in peace."

A demure little moppet told me her favorite carol was "Old Cumalye, faithful." Who was Old Cumalye? Jesus' dog, of course.

An obviously more knowledgeable second grade tyke sang these lyrics to me: "We three kings safari ain't are, bearing gifts we trap us a fire." When I mentioned that those words didn't make much sense, he said: "I know. But it rhymes and things that rhyme don't have to make sense."

Here are a couple of other lyrical lapses that I wouldn't have noticed if I hadn't tape recorded them:

"Peace on the earth, good wilted men, from heaven's all grey shuckings."

" 'Dark the hair,' old angels sing. 'Glo, return the newborn King.' "

Santa certainly came in for his share of comments. Here are four of my favorites:

"Santa Claus was born in the family branch of the Christmas tree."

"Santa lives just north of the imagination."
"He always has fatness and not just skinny bones."
"Clauses are found in both sentences and Santas."
Samuel Butler, the seventeenth century author, once remarked that, "Great actions are not always true sons of great and mighty resolutions." Still, to many grade school youngsters, New Year's Day would be quite hollow without some resolutions. One lad wrote: "I only made one New Year's resolution. I resolved to always finish everything I start because

(By way of explanation, he told me the bell rang at that awkward moment.)

Here's an encouraging report: "Last year I broke my record for keeping New Year's resolutions. I kept one for 26 days."

The problem of which comes first, Christmas or New Year's Day, is more perplexing to some members of the grade school set than the chicken or egg puzzle. Here's a logical explanation: "New Year's Day comes first in the life of a calendar, but Christmas comes first in the life of a person."

Additional thoughts on the subject:

"Christmas just barely sneaks in the nick of time before every new year. We try to hurry it up along about Halloween."

"I observed New Year's Day last year. What I observed was that New Year's Day comes quite late in the night."

"Another good reason for New Year's Eve is to tell the year to get ready to end. When a year or anything else gets to an ending place, it should know enough to stop there and end."

Okay, I can take a hint.

Harold Dunn

Asleep

30

Pale, in the luminous wake of a star,
You lie asleep with your fingers curled
In a puppy dog's fur, unaware that you are
The light of a life, and the hope of the world.

Mary Wright Lamb

Those Short Happy Years

31

Every father has looked at his young, glorying in their youth and sighing for it, too. He has sighed for it because no season is at once so radiant and so short. If the young do not suspect this, their parents realize it. Day by day they see their children's childish days slip through their fingers. Doubtless, none of them would, even if they could, halt time. Certainly they should not endeavor to do so. Still those cuddly, dependent days of faith and discovery slip by as swiftly as if they were minutes.

The period is brief when, to his son, a father walks the earth as a sage, a chief justice, a guide to undreamed-of vistas, a center of trust, and a friend whose word is not questioned, even if his authority is. Yet, brief as that period is, it is glorious. And all the more touching because of the confidence that goes with it. Soon, of course, this confidence will be transferred, and the center of authority move on—to the boy on the next block, the teacher in school, the counselor at camp, and an ever-growing line of legitimate successors. There is no stopping its removal. There is only the fervent trust that the companionship will remain.

John Mason Brown

Sign in a Local Barbershop:

32

Notice to Mothers:
You cut off his curls,
then bring him in;
we'll have the courage
to finish the trim.

Marcelene Cox

Evening Song

33

When children are cross
and my nerves are frayed thinner,
And home from his toil
treads my weary breadwinner,
The thing I want most
in a man—is his dinner!

Sibyl Krausz

Classroom Classics

34

Asked if she could spell Mississippi,
my neighbor's third-grade daughter replied:
"I can spell it,
I just don't know when to stop."

Joseph F. Morris

31

Observer: Don't Make the Kids Do It All

With the beginning of school, it is extremely important for the parent to get organized. The well-organized parent begins by laying in a siege supply of school equipment. The basic supply kit must include:

A loose-leaf binder and a pair of pliers to repair the rings when they get out of alignment. Five hundred sheets of loose-leaf paper. Fifteen hundred loose-leaf-paper-hole reinforcements to repair the holes after they have been gouged by out-of-alignment loose-leaf binder rings.

An eraser. (Caution: Make sure the eraser is too big to fit into the ear and too hard to make for palatable chewing, but not so hard that it is indigestible.)
A half-dozen lead pencils. (Caution: Hard leads are difficult to wash off the parlor wall and more likely than the soft-lead point to inflict painful injuries when left point-upright between the sofa cushions.)

A ruler. A pencil sharpener. A ballpoint pen and five refills. A flexible plastic case which can hold reinforcements, eraser, lead pencils, ruler, pencil sharpener, ballpoint pen and refills, so that everything may be lost simultaneously.

Five book covers which can be easily inscribed with such expressions of the young inquiring mind as "Bored of Education." Optional equipment includes crayons, dividers, T-squares, slide rules and similar accessories for defacing gouged loose-leaf paper or stabbing desks when the student needs emotional release from monotony.

For his own use, the well-organized parent must buy a six-by-three-foot blackboard. The blackboard should be mounted some place conspicuous—over the kitchen stove or in the front hall.

Each child must be compelled to write his homework assignment on the blackboard upon arriving home from school, so that the parent may check it off at bedtime. Each child must also keep an up-to-date record of his whereabouts on the blackboard at all times. In this way, when the child loses his flexible plastic reinforcements-eraser-pencil-ruler-ballpoint-pen-and-refills container, the parent will know where to reach him so that he can be reminded to get a bank loan and buy replacements before the banks close.

Of course, the well-organized parent will not let the blackboard become a mere symbol of drudgery. He will keep it exciting with a succession of bulletins, such as "In view of last night's total homework failure, the transistor batteries have been hidden for the next seven days," or "Little Klaus's Rolling Stones records are hereby confiscated until he stops sticking lead pencils into the electrical outlets."

The well-organized parent does not treat school as if it were his child's problem alone. School is a two-way street. Each quarter of the school year, the parent foregoes one cocktail hour and goes to the P.T.A.'s openhouse at school.

Parents with no system fritter away these evenings hating the paint that is hanging in festoons from the ceiling and badgering the art teacher to give them one good reason why she thinks finger painting is going to help Klaus get into Princeton. The well-organized parent, by contrast, quietly sizes up the teachers.

That Mr. Seltzer in Geography, for example. Does he look like the type who will moon away half the term with a chorus girl, then abandon his class to sell real estate and leave Little Klaus in the clutches of the hard-marking Miss Plimpton, as Mr. Shackley did in Social Studies last year? If Seltzer seems risky, Klaus should be taken out of his class immediately and given to a teacher who will stay with him no matter how miserable the pay.

To swing any weight at the principal's office, of course, the parent must be recognized as a person of substance. It will do little good to walk in unknown and say, "I'm Mr. Schlump and I really wish you'd change Klaus's Geography teacher." Principals enjoy few things as much as refusing to accommodate the world's Schlumps.

The well-organized parent will establish a beachhead during the P.T.A. open-discussion period, perhaps by asking the principal what can be done about "underachievement." Principals love to talk about "underachievement" and are impressed by people who encourage them to.

This sets the stage for a successful appearance at the principal's office with the suggestion that "Since Little Klaus is underachieving with Mr. Seltzer he probably needs a change of teachers." It's not completely honorable, admittedly, but the well-organized parent can scarcely leave his child in the hands of malcontents like Seltzer who think teaching should reimburse them sufficiently to court actresses.

Finally, the well-organized parent is always ready to stimulate the child's thirst for learning by setting the example of his own zeal. In a crisis, he can say, "Look here, this new math isn't hard. I've learned it myself. Take the number 357. All you have to do is quit thinking of it as plain old 357 and think of it as three 100's, five tens and seven ones. Don't you see how sensible it is?"

If the child doesn't, the parent is ready with a fuller explanation. "After school tomorrow," he will explain, "ask the teacher to go over it with you again." Organization—that's all it takes.

Russell Baker

Lines to Four Small Children

36

I often am inclined to think
That it would be much wiser
To give *myself* the vitamins
And *you* the tranquilizer.

Janet Henry

37

A child that is loved has many names.

Hungarian Proverb

Hey, Mom!

38

"Hey, Mom! The sky bowl spilled today
And all the blue poured on the sea!"
Thus, with one young, perceptive thought,
He gave a summer day to me.

"Hey, Mom! God whipped the clouds to cream
And made them stand in little peaks.
I wish that I could reach and taste!"
Oh, lovely are the words he speaks!

One day he held a butterfly,
Then showed me gold dust from its wings.
The touch of Time will brush away
The miracle of simple things.

My son, when you will have outgrown
The wonder of a world so new,
I pray that you will have a child,
For he will teach it back—to you.

Beulah Fenderson Smith

Love Is Not a Trip to the Stars

39

My daughter, you came to me and asked me the question that girls have asked since there have been girls on the earth: "Mother, what is love, and how will I know if it's real?" My first impulse was to smile and give you one of the old, flippant, standby answers—"Love is an ocean of emotion surrounded by expense," or "Love is an itch you can't scratch." But the earnestness in your eyes stopped me. Finally, when I had to say something, I said, "When it's real, nobody will have to label it for you."

Loydean Thomas

Seventeen

40

When a girl is seventeen,
  she's ready
To wear eye shadow and to go
  steady,
To speak with authority on
  Proust,
And boast of the pounds she
  has reduced.

She's ready now to make
  friends with danger,
Including heartbreak and
  Farley Granger,
To lead the march at the
  senior prom,
And explain the facts of life
  to mom.

Georgie Starbuck Galbraith

Lucinda

41

Lucinda in her first long dress
   Is a different girl entirely;
Her voice is low, her smile serene,
   Her eyes dream bright and fiery.

Lucinda in an evening gown,
   Though sipping soda pop with me,
Is Rebecca in a silken robe,
   Walking by the sea.

And I who watch adoring her,
   An ordinary crew-cut lad,
Would give the world if I could be
   Her Lancelot or Galahad.

Barbara Shook Conklin

Compensation

42

I muse as I pay
The tuition deposit:
We're losing a daughter,
But gaining a closet.

Irma Blackford Tierney

43

An advertising executive noticed that his daughter,
returning from Sunday School, clutched a pamphlet.
"What's that you have there?" he asked.
"Oh," she replied, "just an ad about heaven."

Claribel C. Heinen

44

Father to teen-age boy:
"You should run for Congress, Sheldon.
You're very good at introducing
new bills in the house!"

Bernard Lansky

Familiar Stranger

45

Mother looked up at her oldest son,
Now come of age with twenty-one;
Birthdays filling him out to size,
But sons stay small in mothers' eyes.
Then she gazed downward through the years,
The months of joy, the days of tears,
The marks on the door that told how tall,
The cowboy wallpaper on the wall;
That day she felt her hair turn gray,
When he and Rover ran away;
But both were there for bedtime prayer,
And the gold came back into her hair.
Remembered his slam-bang, "See ya, Mom!"
Straightened his tie for the junior prom.
She raised her eyes again to scan
Her son, and saw a strange, new man.

Ralph W. Seager

Poor Grandma!

46

Grandfather lost his hearing aid;
He really doesn't mind it;
Let the grandchildren shriek,
And stay all week,
When they go home, he'll find it.

Madeleine Laeufer

The Expectant Grandfather's Guidebook

47

Some people seem to think it's easy to be a grandfather. Well, perhaps so, but I found a surprising variety of pitfalls surrounding the job. Since I am now three months along, I feel it my duty to give some advice and guidance to men approaching this honorable estate.

Face up to the facts of life. When my son and daughter-in-law announced the approaching event, my wife and I were thrilled, of course, and the four of us had a big evening of celebration. But after the kids had gone home, a reaction set in. "Why, you're too young to be a grandfather," I said to myself. This was obviously untrue—I was 55. "Well, you don't *look* old enough," I said. This was even more ridiculous.

The truth is, the march of time is beyond our power to alter. So, accept and enjoy it.

Don't lose your cool. My wife has an infallible technique for spreading news. She telephones certain girl friends, pledges them to secrecy, then tells them the latest bulletin. Up to now the fastest-moving, hottest items have been surgical details. But I discovered that word of an impending grandchild is hotter still.

The very next afternoon I found myself the center of attention. My niece and several of her playmates (fractious ten-year-olds) spotted me half a block off and yelled in unison, "Hey, Grandpa!" Then they burst into giggles, jumping up and down and covering their mouths with their hands.

I had just escaped these moppets when the village cop drove slowly past, stuck his head out the patrol-car window, removed the cigar from his mouth and called, "Hey, Grandpa!"

Then that evening I found my wife looking at me with amusement and affection. She said gently, "Hey, Grandpa."

How can one keep his cool under these conditions? I have evolved a facial expression which I recommend to all men. When you're kidded, don't try to defend yourself; simply give an enigmatic smile that is ever so slightly touched with pride and modesty. Let them figure *that* out.

Avoid a sex preference. I wanted a boy, a grandson, not only for pride of name but because I'd know how to handle one. My only child was a boy and how well I remembered the various and dismaying behavior patterns he went through. Now I'd be able to stand at his shoulder to advise and reassure. "This will pass," I'd say to him. "He's acting exactly as you did at his age. Be firm, but not alarmed."

Well, she arrived on schedule, weighing six pounds ten ounces and carrying the name Jennifer. When my son telephoned me from the hospital with the news I felt a small stab of disappointment. But that afternoon when I looked through the nursery window at my granddaughter I discovered I had been wrong, completely and totally wrong—I had wanted Jennifer from the beginning. This tiny creature, so delicate and feminine, was already a mystery. No one would expect any advice from me on how to raise or discipline *her.* I was freed of all responsibilities except to love and indulge her.

Get yourself a specialty. There will be competition in the family to handle and care for the baby and, frankly, there just aren't jobs to go around. It is well for the grandfather to find some area where his services are unique. I chose photography. I reasoned that everyone would want a complete picture record of the child—asleep, awake, first smile, first tooth, first step. The "court photographer" becomes the indispensable man.

The day after I heard of the pregnancy I went to our village photo shop to buy a simple camera. I emerged an hour later. Around my neck hung an expensive reflex camera with through-the-lens light metering, diaphragm stops down to f 1.4, shutter speed up to a thousandth of a second. In a leather gadget bag hung from my shoulder there nestled auxiliary lenses, filters and an electronic flash gun. I had a good six months to practice.

When Jennifer arrived I was ready. At the first opportunity, I was in position in front of the nursery window, inserting a roll of high-speed color film in my camera, adjusting knobs, firing my flash gun.

It was five days before I discovered that disaster was awaiting me. After finishing the roll of film, I opened the camera to remove it—and stared in disbelief. In loading the camera I had not properly attached the film to the take-up reel, and it had come loose. I had no pictures of Jennifer! What an ignominious beginning of my career as court photographer!

Fortunately, failure becomes a goad that forces redoubled efforts. I now have boxes and boxes of color slides showing Jennifer in all her lovely and fragile innocence. When friends congratulate me on the pictures, I say, with becoming modesty, "No photographer could go wrong with such an enchanting model." And maybe that's true.

Be patient with Grandma. Of all the adults involved, the one who will have the most difficulty adjusting to a new role will be Grandma, your wife. She is delighted to be a grandmother, but she wants it on her terms. During this period she is apt to say totally opposite things and not see any contradiction.

"Do you suppose they'll let us baby-sit much?" she said one evening. "No doubt *her* mother will see more of the baby than I will."

Minutes later she said, "I don't want them to get the idea that we're always available to baby-sit at their beck and call. I have my own life to live, too."

A grandfather must be careful not to agree (or disagree) with everything she says during this period. To find yourself stuck with one of her discarded positions can be a nerve-racking experience.

Learn to be a liar. This advice may sound indefensible, but there are times when it is the only way to secure your rights.

Jennifer was a month old when she first came to spend the whole day with us. I had it all figured out—which jobs were appropriately done by the grandmother and which by the grandfather. For instance, changing diapers is obviously woman's work, while pushing the buggy is just as surely a task for a man.

We had Jennifer in our possession for a full 20 minutes before we decided it was time to give the neighbors a chance to admire her. We bundled her up, put her in the buggy and tucked a blanket firmly around her. Then my wife grabbed the buggy handle and shoved off.

"Hey, wait a minute," I called. "That's *my* job, pushing the buggy."

"No, dear," she said sweetly. "The job belongs to whoever gets hold of the handle first."

I was shocked. In 30 years of marriage, I'd never suspected my wife of such sneakiness.

Later that day, after the triumphal neighborhood tour, one feeding, one nap and four diaper changes, my wife said, "Let's go downtown. I want to buy Jennifer a dress."

The three of us piled into the car. Downtown, I found a parking space, turned off the motor, put coins in the meter, then opened the car door for my wife. "Here, I'll hold Jennifer while you get out. Then I'll give her back to you."

I cradled Jennifer in my arms and began a slow parade down the street.

"Wait," my wife called. "You said you'd give her back to me."

"Now what do you suppose would make me tell a lie like that?"

Conform—don't try to change the rules. The rituals of grandfatherhood were established generations ago and nothing you can do will change them. Though you be a soldier, tycoon, explorer or Phi Beta Kappa, folklore has it that the grandchild will bedazzle you, rob you of your senses, reduce you to a jellylike blob of emotion. And folklore is correct.

You are *expected* to boast. Why not do so? You are *expected* to see your grandchild as the most beautiful and smartest baby ever born. Why try to be modest? For the first time in your life you are *expected* to indulge yourself. So don't knock the system.

That's all the time I have for advice—there's a car coming up the driveway bringing Jennifer for a visit. She knows me now and always greets me with a smile of incandescent radiance. Her parents and her grandmother claim it is the same smile she gives them, but I know the difference. Jennifer and I know the difference.

Floyd Miller

Walking with Grandma

48

I like to walk with Grandma;
Her steps are short like mine.
She doesn't say, "Now hurry up,"
She always takes her time.

I like to walk with Grandma;
Her eyes see things mine do—
Wee pebbles bright, a funny cloud,
Half-hidden drops of dew.

Most people have to hurry;
They do not stop and see.
I'm glad that God made Grandmas
Unrushed and young like me!

Mildred R. Grenier

43

49

Queen Mother Elizabeth:
The World's Most Famous Grandmother

Where Prince Charles (of Great Britain) is concerned, nothing is too good or too much trouble for his grandmother. She was at a dinner once where there was a display of magic. Afterward she asked the magician about a trick in which pennies are made to appear one by one in a closed hand.

"Please show me how it's done," she said. "I want to show my grandson."

She practiced until she had perfected it, then surprised Charles and (Princess) Anne with it. Like Oliver Twist, they begged for more. So the Queen Mum learned more tricks. Today she is a fairly accomplished amateur magician!

"But I simply can't keep up with the demand," she has said jokingly.

It was "Granny" who sat beside Prince Charles in gray old Westminster Abbey when his mother was crowned queen, and quietly explained this 750-year-old ceremony in which he will one day play the leading role. But the young prince was more interested in the brilliantine which had been used to make his rather unruly hair stay in place. He ran his fingers through his hair and pushed them under the Queen Mother's nose. "Smell, Granny," he urged. "Doesn't it smell nice?"

Another time he was sucking candy as he drove with her in one of the royal cars. As the car drew to a standstill, he remembered one of the rules of royalty which had been painstakingly drilled into him—never appear in public with anything in your mouth.

"Hold that for me, please, Granny," he said, taking the candy from his mouth and popping it, still wet and sticky into her gloved hand.

While there is much about the young prince's serious, painstaking demeanor that is reminiscent of his mother, there is even more that is a reminder of his grandmother. He is generous, thoughtful and patient—all facets of the Queen Mother's character.

"A very warmhearted boy," the Queen Mum herself has called him.

It was (Princess) Anne who paid the Queen Mum the highest compliment. She was having an English lesson in the schoolroom which forms part of the royal nursery at Buckingham Palace. Anne had been asked to define the word "charming."

She hesitated only momentarily. "Someone like Granny," she announced.

Ralphe M. White

50

The children will not leave unless I do.
I shall not leave unless their father does,
and the King will not leave the country
in any circumstances whatever.

Elizabeth, Queen Mother of England.
Reported answer to press query regarding
the Princesses' leaving England
after the bombing of Buckingham Palace in 1940

51

Drink the brimming cup of life
to the full and to the end—
and thank God and nature
for its trials and challenges,
its punishments and rewards,
its gifts of beauty,
wisdom, labor and love.

Will Durant

Chapter Two

Live in Deeds, Not Years

We live in deeds, not years; in thoughts, not breaths;
In feelings not in figures on a dial.
We should count time by heart-throbs. He most lives
Who thinks most—feels the noblest—acts the best.

Philip James Bailey

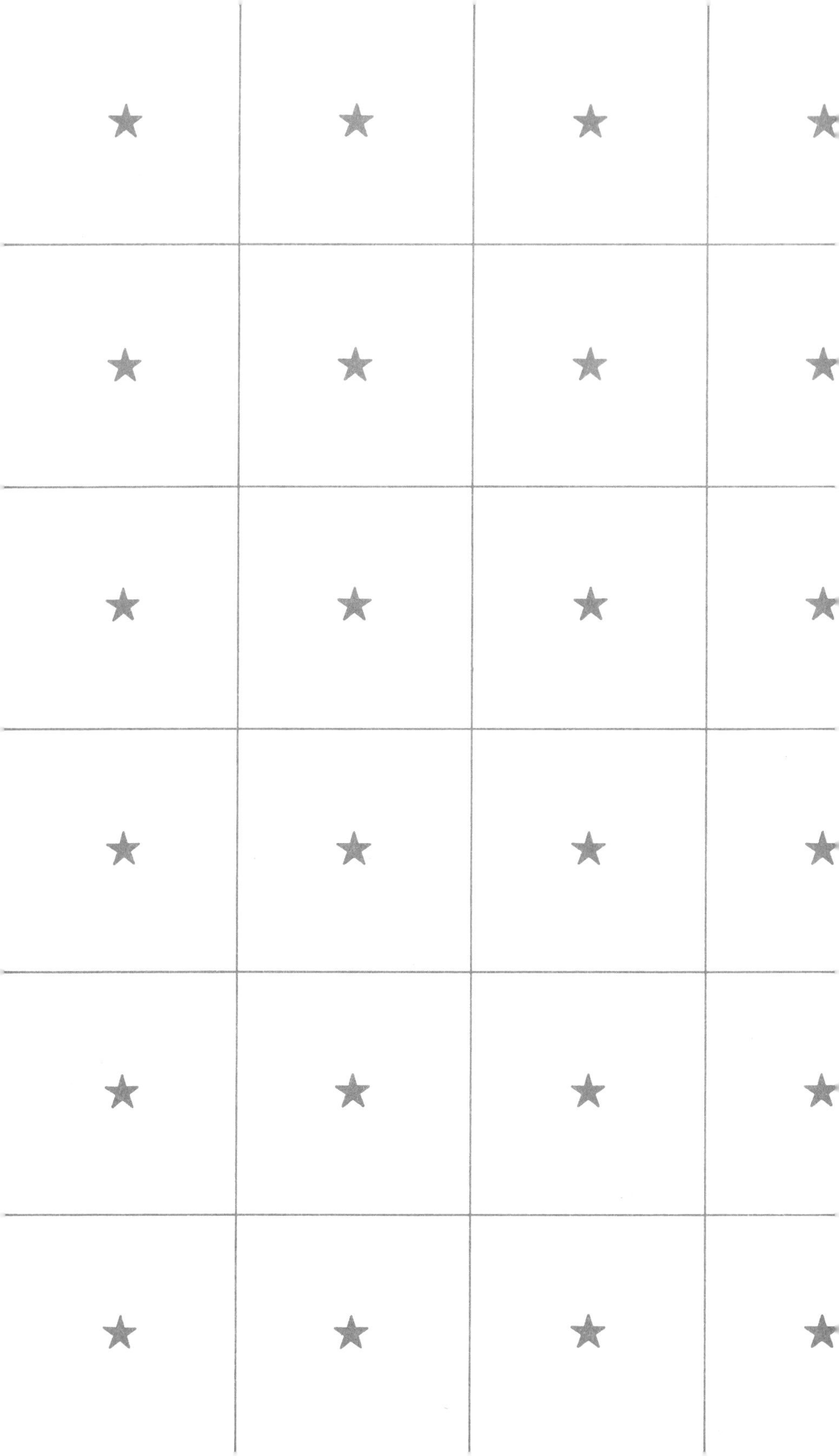

53 God, give me hills to climb,
And strength for climbing!

Arthur Guiterman

Jimmy and His Cowboy Belt

54 Two or three days before Christmas last year, a group of children who come often to our house for stories on Monday afternoons, came and we sat in a small room around a little Franklin stove in which a welcome fire was burning. We sat there and we talked about Christmas. I was aware that there was a shine from the firelight in the eyes of those boys and girls and on their wind-polished cheeks.

But no shine equalled that which gleamed from the buckle on the cowboy belt that Jimmy was wearing. Nine-year-old Jimmy was something of a swaggerer, but he liked books and liked to come and listen to stories. I had known for a long time that his cowboy belt was a prized possession, and the buckle was something marvelous.

We talked about Christmas for a little while. And then I read them one of the loveliest stories I know—Rachel Field's "All Through The Night"—a simple retelling of the Christmas story. There was a great silence while I read—the only sounds the words of the ageless tale and the crackling of the fire in the stove.

When the story was over, no one spoke for a moment. I knew that it could not be a long moment, because something like that can't be held very long—with fifteen or twenty children for whom the deliciousness of Christmas is only two days away.

I was the first one, however, to break the spell with words other than the story. I said, "What if we put on our coats and hats and went out of this little house and across the field in the snow and, dark as it is, went down the slope, across the brook, and into the woods? What if there we came upon the stable and the manger and the Baby? What could we give to him?"

Again there was a moment of utter silence. Then Jimmy put his hand on his middle and said, "I'd give him my cowboy belt."

Elizabeth Yates

Tell the Children

55

Would you set your name among the stars?
Then write it large upon the hearts of children.
They will remember!

Have you visions of a finer, happier world?
Tell the children!
They will build it for you.

Have you a word of hope for poor, blind,
stumbling human kind?
Then give it not to stupid, blundering men.
Give it to the children.
In their clear, untroubled minds it will
reflect itself a thousandfold
And some day paint itself upon the mountain tops.
Somewhere a Lincoln plays and learns and
watches with bewildered gaze
This strange procession of mismannered souls.

Have you a ray of light to offer him?
Then give it, and some day it will help
To make the torch which he will use
To light the world to freedom and to joy.

Clare Tree Major

56

It is better to live one day as a lion
than a hundred years as a sheep.

Italian Proverb

57

One hour of life,
crowded to the full with glorious action,
and filled with noble risk, is worth whole years
of those mean observances of paltry decorum,
in which men steal through existence,
like sluggish waters through a marsh,
without either honour or observation.

Sir Walter Scott

58

It is no use to wait for your ship to come in,
unless you have sent one out.

Belgian Proverb

59

Happiness in this world, when it comes, comes incidentally. Make it the object of pursuit, and it leads us a wild-goose chase, and is never attained. Follow some other object, and very possibly we may find that we have caught happiness without dreaming of it; but likely enough it is gone the moment we say to ourselves, "Here it is!" like the chest of gold that treasure-seekers find.

Nathaniel Hawthorne

60

Too low they build, who build beneath the stars.

Edward Young

Forty Is Forty

61

When you get down to brass tacks, forty is forty. Take those Job Opportunity ads that say "Women over forty need not apply." Even if you had no intention of applying, it stings. Almost every cosmetic house features nourishing facial creams, specifically created for women forty and over. The Junior League disengages its members when they reach forty and, by an odd coincidence, the Young Republicans and Young Democrats use the same dividing line.

Hair rinses and hormone creams are helpful in their way, but forty is still no joke. The only thing I can say in its favor is that it beats thirty-nine—which *is* a joke. At thirty-nine you are subjected to a barrage of low humor ("You and Jack Benny, huh?") and people peer at you suspiciously as they try to figure out how old you *really* are. Thirty-nine should be skipped, like the thirteenth floor in hotels. At least when you admit to forty, no one suspects you of lying about your age.

No one suspects you of anything else either. My best friend blithely suggested that her husband take me out to dinner when my husband was out of town. And off she skipped to her Spanish class, secure in the knowledge that her husband was in safe hands.

A fortieth birthday is the moment of truth, and a rude awakening it is. You emerge from slumber with a vague feeling of depression which you can't pin down. Then you remember. It's your birthday! Quaking with apprehension, you check to see if you've developed liver spots overnight, and relief washes over you as you realize that nothing so drastic has occurred. You look and feel about the same as you did yesterday—which isn't saying much, since you haven't worn a two-piece swimsuit for some time now, and you haven't been able to look up a telephone number without glasses for years.

But the plain fact is, you don't *feel* forty. How in the world did you get so old so young? Why, you don't even feel grown-up, much less mature. Where are the wisdom and character you'd expected to acquire by this time? What happened to the tact and sophistication you should have picked up over the years? Where, for that matter, is the nest egg you should have salted away and the portfolio of stocks you'd planned to secure? Here you are, clearly retarded for your age. Just a forty-year-old mixed-up kid.

Painfully sensitive about your own age, you become acutely conscious of everyone else's, and you discover that most people are younger than you are. This is logical enough, but it's a shock—especially when an authority figure like a school principal or a surgeon turns out to be your junior. How can you have any confidence in the diagnosis of a mere broth of a boy whose diploma, framed right there on the wall, proclaims that he graduated from medical school the year your second child started kindergarten? It's even worse when you look around you and discover that the world is being run by juveniles. After you've spent the better part of your life looking up to judges and Cabinet members as mature, dignified individuals whose age and wisdom commanded respect, it comes as a jolt to realize that Congress is full of rosy-cheeked striplings and the President is *not* old enough to be your father.

It becomes increasingly evident that you have been around for some time. All the jokes you hear sound vaguely familiar, and half the people you meet remind you of someone else you've seen before.

One of the checkers at my neighborhood supermarket looks exactly like Mrs. McMillan, who was postmistress at the beach where we spent summers when I was a child. What I mean is, the checker looks the way Mrs. McMillan looked *then.* I saw Mrs. McMillan last summer, and now *she* looks like Grandma Moses....

Upsetting as it is to find yourself facing it, there *is* a life after forty. What's to be done about it? What is the secret of perpetual middle age? The trick, I suspect, is to burn that bridge when you come to it. You can't just sit there, lamenting your lost youth and plucking out your gray hairs. You've got to develop a positive attitude, however little there is to be positive *about.*

To prove that my heart's in the right place, I have a couple of pieces of mildly constructive advice:

Don't pretend that you don't care how you look. When you're a sweet young thing with roses in your cheeks, you can admit winsomely that you don't use anything on your face but plain soap and water. If you're a mere slip of a girl who looks fetching in a bikini, it's cute to confess that you're the world's worst glutton. But, at forty, ingenuousness loses its charm. If you admit that you eat like a horse, the response you'll get is a nod, meaning, "So *that* explains it."

Don't embroider your age on your bib. I don't exactly advocate lying about it. That's every woman's own personal decision. (In my own case, it's impossible. I still live in the city where I was born, and I'm surrounded by people who can, and do, recall when I was graduated from Lincoln High School.)

In any case, honesty does not compel you to reminisce about the first ninety days of the Roosevelt Administration or the time you saw Ruby Keeler in *42nd Street.*

Try to remember not to call the refrigerator the icebox or the stereo the phonograph, and try to forget that you ever heard of the NRA, Joe Penner and Ella Cinders.

Why these remnants of the misty past should remain crystal clear in my mind, I don't know. Especially since I can't remember where I put the car keys five minutes ago. But that's forty for you.

Jane Goodsell

Nobody Knows the Quandaries I've Seen—

62

I was born too late. Perhaps I might have made a better adjustment in some bygone era when life was less complicated. The Stone Age? Too outdoorsy. The Renaissance? No, I couldn't live without my portable hair drier. Contrariwise, there are some things I can't live *with* in this bedazzling century. Particularly, making decisions.

I'm not talking about decisions on the farm problem, or the admission of Red China to the U.N. What bewilders me is peanut butter—whether to buy chunky style or creamy style. The creamy type is nice because it's so smooth and—well, creamy. But on the other hand, the chunky style has a good, crunchy texture, so maybe....

I'd forget the whole thing and buy honey, but then I'd have to decide between the jar, the carton, the comb and the squeeze bottle.

Worst of all are those lovely decorator colors. Everything from ball-point pens to dustpans now comes in eight assorted shades—and I love each and every one of them! Someday I'll go to pieces right in the middle of the supermarket. I'll be standing at the paper-products counter, trying to decide between aqua- and peach-colored roller towels, and suddenly something inside me will snap and I'll throw myself on the floor and sob.

I've got problems with my electric blanket, too. Position 3 on the dial seems comfortable... but mightn't 4 be just a teensy bit cozier? Or maybe 2 would be preferable for all-night sleeping comfort. Some nights, as I lie awake fiddling with the control, it seems to me I had an easier time back when I was faced with only two choices: (1) curl up in a ball; or (2) get up and rummage around for an extra blanket.

Life was simple in those days. Stockings didn't come in proportioned sizes, and washing-machine dials had two settings: *on* and *off*. Telephones were black, pillow slips white, you could count the types of breakfast cereal on your fingers, and six delicious flavors of ice cream were a many-splendored variety.

Some people, of course, have lightning reflexes and firm convictions. Recently, I was leaning against a bakery counter, chin propped on hands, trying to decide whether I wanted potato bread, buttercrust, egg twist (topped with poppy seeds, or sesame seeds, or plain), sour-dough French, hearth-baked French, Vienna bread, oatmeal bread, pumpernickel, orange-nut or cinnamon—and whether I wanted it in a small loaf or large, unsliced, thin-sliced or regular. As the salesclerk drummed her fingers on the counter, this other woman marched in, swept a glance over the dizzying array on the shelves, and announced that she wanted a small loaf of egg twist with poppy seeds, unsliced.

Now *there's* a woman who is master of her fate. I'll bet *she* has no trouble deciding whether to set her alarm clock *loud* or *soft*.

I know I ought to be a child of my century—brisk, decisive, firm. But I'm not built that way. Last week, bristling with determination, I walked into an ice-cream shop featuring 26 flavors. I would make my choice in a cool, adult, authoritative manner; I wouldn't even look at the flavor chart to see what Today's Special might be; I wouldn't panic. Thus steeled, I asked for a quart of vanilla.

The counter girl clicked to attention. "Plain or French vanilla?" she asked.

"Uh—plain," I said.
"Regular or low-calorie?"
"Regular."
"Soft or hard-frozen?"
I clenched my fists. "Soft. No, I mean hard!"
"Brick or hand packed?"
And that's when I went out of focus. I strode over to the ice-cream freezer, grabbed a carton and bleated, "I'll take this!"
And I don't even *like* licorice ripple!

Jane Goodsell

63

Today well-lived,
makes every yesterday a dream of happiness
and every tomorrow a vision of hope.

Oliver Wendell Holmes

64

There is no cure for birth or death
save to enjoy the interval.

Santayana

65

Half the joy of life is in little things taken on the run.
Let us run if we must—even the sands do that—
but let us keep our hearts young and our eyes open
that nothing worth our while shall escape us.
And everything is worth its while
if we only grasp it and its significance.

Victor Cherbuliez

Father's Day

66

Moments when a woman admires the father of her young:

Sunday mornings when he gathers the littlest ones on his lap or the arms of a chair, and in his own chipper, comic way reads them the funnies...

When he tells a worried youngster: "Now don't fret about that test, just go in there and do the best you can."...

When he backs up another who's in a jam: "Just tell the truth and you'll be okay. C'mon, I'll go with you to explain."...

When, groaning but game, he agrees to take on another office in the Scouts or PTA...

When you see him contriving safety devices for windows, scouring the yard for glass or nails, testing new toys for possible hazards, and firmly fixing anything that could go wrong...

When you hear his hammer banging away in the basement late at night, building a playhouse for your little girl...

When he hastens home from the office early to help with a birthday party...

When he adds an extra ten to the check he's sending a child away at school...

When he piles not only his own flock but several extras into the car to take to an amusement park. And when their mothers come rushing out with money, he grandly shoos them off...

When, dead for sleep, he snoozes fitfully on the davenport, waiting for that teen-age party to be over so he can pick up the kids and drive them home...

When you surprise him quietly going through his old suits, and discover he's hoping to make them last another season so that all the rest of you can have new clothes...

When you see him laboring over accounts spread across the dining room table, and know that he's striving to keep up the insurance, manage money for college educations, make sound investments for the future, and balance a badly strained budget—and all without causing you too much concern.

They're not glamorous, any of these things. They probably never entered your head when you were canoeing with him in the moonlight, yelling him on to make that winning touchdown, or dancing with him at a prom. But they're the things that really count. The things that fill your heart when the man you married becomes the man you honor on Father's Day.

Marjorie Holmes

Earth Is Enough

67

We men of Earth here have the stuff
Of Paradise—we have enough!
We need no other stones to build
The Temple of the Unfulfilled—
No other ivory for the doors—
No other marble for the floors—
No other cedar for the beam
And dome of man's immortal dream.

Here on the paths of every-day—
Here on the common human way
Is all the stuff the gods would take
To build a Heaven, to mold and make
New Edens. Ours the stuff sublime
To build Eternity in time!

Edwin Markham

68

May you live all the days of your life.

Jonathan Swift

69

Far away there in the sunshine
are my highest aspirations.
I may not reach them,
but I can look up and see their beauty,
believe in them,
and try to follow where they lead.

Louisa May Alcott

70

No one ever gets very far
unless he accomplishes the impossible
at least once a day.

Elbert Hubbard

After Polio ... the Way It Was

71

When I came home to New York from Groton for the holidays that first Christmas after Father was stricken with polio, I dreaded the thought of seeing him lying in bed, a cripple.

I needn't have. Pa saw to that.

I went in to his room, striving manfully to assume an air of nonchalance, even gaiety, so as not to let him know how I really felt. Remember, I was a solemn, earnest young gentleman of fourteen—indoctrinated in the Groton code and brought up not to show emotions.

Pa read me like a book, and he worked a small miracle for me. He was propped up on pillows, and those trapezes and rings over his bed on which he already was exercising his upper body upset me a bit. Pa instantly made me forget it. His chin still stuck out and he was grinning and he stretched out his arms to me. "Come here, old man," he said.

61

I rushed over and received his embrace, and I learned right then and there that whatever had happened to his legs had not affected the power in his arms. Then, even though I was a Roosevelt and a Grotonian, I cried a bit, but, with Pa squeezing me and slapping me on the back and carrying on enthusiastically on how "grand" I looked, I soon was chattering right along with him, telling him all about Old Peabody—only I didn't call him (the Headmaster) that—and the football team and prospects for spring baseball.

That very Christmas—only four and a half months after polio—Father was getting down on the floor to exercise. He had been Indian wrestling with Elliott, Franklin, and Johnny, and now with me home he had some competition nearer his size.

"You think you can take the Old Man?" he challenged me. "Well, just get down here and try it!" His grip was so strong he could make me yell, and he beat me every time. We went from Indian wrestling to more vigorous forms of rough-housing.

I still don't know how he did it, but Father kept us almost completely at ease. Even that first Christmas when he could move only the upper half of his body, he gave the impression of mobility. He cushioned the shock for us. I know he made it possible for me to participate in various festivities that Christmas without feeling any depression or guilt.

James Roosevelt

72

There are many ways of going forward,
but there is only one way of standing still.

Franklin Delano Roosevelt

73

Whether a man accepts from Fortune her spade
and will look downward and dig,
or from Aspiration her axe and cord,
and will scale the ice,
the one and only success
which it is his to command
is to bring to his work a mighty heart.

Oliver Wendell Holmes

74

To the man who himself strives earnestly,
God also lends a helping hand.

Aeschylus

75

Man is soul and body,
formed for deeds,
Of high resolve.

Percy Bysshe Shelley

Dad, I Need Some Money

76

To me, one of the most touching gestures a man makes is that old familiar one of reaching into his hip pocket and drawing forth his leather wallet.

"Touching is right!" he'd probably say, laughing, if you mentioned it. For day in and day out, he's being touched for money.

"Dad, this is cracker-money day, and also I've got to have a new notebook."... "Dad, I've got a big date tonight. How about getting my allowance early?"... "Don't forget to leave me some money, dear. The maid's coming today, and I think I'll take advantage of that shoe sale downtown."

Cheerfully, patiently, automatically, he produces that faithful source of supply. Without complaint, he doles it out—the change for the children, the pay for the cleaning woman, the cash you specify. "Now, you sure that's enough? Here's a little extra, just in case."

Sometimes he's forced to protest. If the bank account is low, he has to say so. But you know that it hurts him to do so, and he'll put it off as long as he can. He'd far rather cut corners and do without himself than deny his family the things they need or would like to have. For he cherishes that age-old American tribute—"a good provider." To be able to take care of his own is a matter of masculine pride.

He also likes to hold up his end of things with other men. How often during the day he reaches for his wallet—to pay a cab fare, pick up the check at lunch, donate to some cause or drive. And then, when he gets home at night, the whole family campaign starts up again: "Honey, the paper boy is at the door."... "There's a man collecting for the Salvation Army."... "Judy's leaving for her music lesson. She'll have to have three dollars for it."

And watching the hand travel to the familiar spot, you realize: "This is the hand that works for us."

And you remember your father's big brown calloused hand making that selfsame journey, to produce an old-fashioned snap purse, from which he brought forth funds. And you think of all the hands of men throughout the country, going back and forth to the hip pocket, like faithful pendulums, in this timeless cause.

"Dad, I need some money." How many billfolds that plea wears out! No wonder husbands so often need new ones for birthdays or Christmas. The billfolds get tired and worn and thin; eventually, they give up.

But the men? Tired and worn though they too may become, somehow they can't just quit, and they seldom give up. They are made of tougher, finer leather, sewed with sinews much too strong. So long as there's life in their bodies and love in their hearts and somebody to say, "Dad, I need some money," they manage to keep on filling the wallets. And reaching for them.

Marjorie Holmes

Great in little Tasks

77

People who are faithful in that which is least wear very radiant crowns. They are the people who are great in little tasks. They are scrupulous in the rutty roads of drudgery. They win triumphs amid small irritations. They are as loyal when wearing aprons in the kitchen as if they wore purple and fine linen in the visible presence of the king.

They finish the most obscure bit of work as if it were to be displayed before an assembled heaven by Him who is the Lord of light and glory. Great souls are those who are faithful in that which is least.

John Henry Jowett

78

I studied the lives of great men and famous women;
and I found that the men and women who got to the top
were those who did the jobs they had in hand,
with everything they had of
energy and enthusiasm and hard work.

Harry S. Truman

79

He that never climbed never fell.

Proverb

80

In Tucson, I know a Navajo silversmith who goes right on creating fine jewelry while most of his competitors have compromised on workmanship and materials by making gewgaws for the tourist trade. One day I asked him why he spent so much time turning out little pieces of art when he could cash in so easily with inferior workmanship.

"I tried making junk," he said. "It was like making false money. It fooled other people, but it didn't fool me. I look at my bankbook maybe once or twice a month. But I have to live with myself every day."

John Kord Lagemann

To Give a Child a Dream

81

You cannot practice for her every day;
The knowledge that you give her will not stream
On her young mind in one bright, blinding ray,–
But you can plant a dream.

Ah, you can plant a dream in her young heart,
A dream of excellence whose light will gleam
Upon her pathway as the years depart,–
Your words can plant a dream.

To sow a dream and see it spread and grow,
To light a lamp and watch its brightness gleam,
Here is a gift that is divine I know–
To give a child a dream.

Anne Campbell

A Young Girl's Gift

82

As I prepared breakfast, the week-before-Christmas treadmill whirled round and round in my head: must do this, must do that...

Only when the eggs and coffee were ready did I realize that my daughter Andrea was still standing by the window in her blue robe, dreamily twisting one long strand of dark-honey hair between her fingers.

"Anything wrong?" I asked.

She jumped a little, as though my voice had recalled her from a dream. "I was just wondering what to wear for the Christmas concert. I can't decide between my red wool and the green taffeta."

Andrea plays the flute in the school orchestra. "Either dress should be fine," I said, wishing she would eat so we could clear the table.

She sat and began to pick at her food slowly. My nerves tightened: had to wrap packages, get to the post office. Masses of silvery paper and bright ribbon awaited me, tags saying From and To, and a red crayon for writing Do Not Open Until Christmas.

When the last package was ready for mailing, I ran upstairs to get my coat. Passing Andrea's room, I stopped in surprise. Although she was no paragon of neatness, it was a long time since she had left her room in such a mess. Her bed was unmade, her bureau cluttered, her closet door ajar. I glanced in, then turned away as I saw a few unwrapped presents on the shelf. But even that quick glance was enough to see that only a fraction of her shopping was accomplished. And where in the world was she now?

I sent Brad to find her. In a minute she appeared, carrying her flute. "I—I was just practicing in the garage," she stammered. She looked around the room vaguely. "Gosh, it needs straightening, doesn't it?"

"That was my feeling," I replied grimly. "And, if I may

venture a guess, a few presents need to be bought."

My feckless child grinned. "Are you hinting for a gift, Mom?" In a ludicrously haughty social voice, she assured me, "You shall not be forgotten, never fear. Night and day I am planning, planning, abrim with yuletide spirit."

As the week progressed, I felt increasingly tired and rushed. The hours began to speed up, like an old movie film. Newspaper ads tolled the countdown: six more, five more, four more shopping days. It was impossible, absolutely out of the question, that I would ever get the last gift bought, the last tag written, the last special meal cooked.

Russ's sense of doom equaled mine. Work was extra heavy at his office. Even Brad began to look harried as he scampered through multitudinous festivities at school and Scouts. Of us all, only Andrea remained buoyant—and small wonder, I thought, since responsibility sat on her so lightly.

I was puzzled, though, by an odd remoteness about her, and she seemed evasive when I questioned why she came home late from school or left unusually early in the morning. Once I heard her whispering on the phone in a voice of suppressed excitement, and caught the words, "No, not an inkling, I'm sure of it."

On one of those last mornings, I decorated and baked Christmas cookies. There were several interruptions, and I slipped farther and farther behind schedule. At noon, with guests coming for lunch, I set about tidying the kitchen. I opened the dishwasher—but it was full already, and not of clean dishes. Andrea had loaded the machine after breakfast and failed to start it.

Tears filled my eyes. Suddenly it all seemed too much: the dirty dishes, the too-tight schedule, Andrea's negligence. Above all, *Christmas* was just too much. It didn't seem worth it.

Depressed and furious, I dumped my mixing bowls into the sink and fixed lunch. When my guests left, I had barely time enough to do all the dishes before picking up Andrea at school to drive her to her flute lesson.

I pulled up at the high school at three o'clock, still seething. Andrea's coltish, long-haired figure detached itself from a group of friends and ran toward me. I almost weakened at the sight of the funny, half-skipping run, left over from her bouncy little-girlhood. She tumbled happily into the car, bubbling with some bit of high-school news. But as she saw my face, her gaiety gave way to sudden apprehension.

"What's wrong?"

I told her. She couldn't remember anything, she was untidy, inconsiderate. "I don't know what you're thinking of, you go dreaming along..." We had nearly reached the music school before I ran out of things to say. Beside me, Andrea sat perfectly quiet. I did not glance at her, but I could imagine the set of that clear young profile; the fixed expression of the wide hazel eyes. When I stopped the car, she got out and walked wordlessly away.

Suddenly I felt sad and ashamed. Did Christmas have to be like this? Responsible for the "success" of the day, I was churning over every detail, trying to make sure nothing was forgotten. Yet something was missing: the dazzling light of a Star in the East, the birth of a miraculous Child... the promise and the wonder had escaped me.

That evening, we rushed through our dinner. It was the night of the high-school Christmas concert. Along with other families, Russ and Brad and I took our seats in the auditorium.

I saw Andrea, in her green taffeta, sit down at her music stand in the pit. Up on the stage, the boys and girls of the chorus massed in a double line. Russ and I smiled; it was the warm, familiar moment of assessment: how tall Johnny Evans was getting, how pretty Susie looked, Caroline Miller had cut her hair....

As the concert started, my tension began to drain away. I listened, relaxed and moved by the special atmosphere that these young people created. Old and new songs about snow and reindeer alternated with reverent Christmas music. Between pieces, we all exchanged contented glances with our neighbors.

At last the music teacher announced the final selection: "Jesu, Joy of Man's Desiring." He added, "For this last number we have a soloist. Because she wanted it to be a surprise for her family, her name is not listed on the program." Smiling, he looked down into the orchestra pit: "Andrea Hill."

I gasped. My tears blurred her image as Andrea rose and, to the applause of that packed auditorium, took her place on the stage in front of the massed chorus. Just before she raised the flute to her lips, she looked straight at her father and brother and me, and gave us a wide, humorless, joyful smile.

I smiled back, tremulous. Russ tucked a handkerchief into my hand. With one accord, we turned to Brad just as he turned to us. Our unity with each other and with the radiant girl on the stage seemed to encircle the four of us, out of all the world.

Did the music sound so beautiful because our child's instrument led it? I don't think so. All the fresh young voices were beautiful, and all the hopeful, shining faces.

But most beautiful of all was the sense of wonder that filled me. I remembered the practicing, out of hearing, in the garage; the extra time spent at school; the details ignored, the little things undone—while she did this big thing. Instinctively wise, Andrea had grasped a truth that had eluded me: that dutifulness is less than love.

With her love, she had presented me, now and forever, with the music and the meaning of Christmas. That was Andrea's gift.

Elizabeth Starr Hill

Hold Fast Your Dreams

83

Hold fast your dreams!
Within your heart
Keep one still, secret spot
Where dreams may go,
And, sheltered so,
May thrive and grow
Where doubt and fear are not.
O keep a place apart,
Within your heart,
For little dreams to go!

Think still of lovely things that are not true.
Let wish and magic work at will in you.
Be sometimes blind to sorrow. Make believe!
Forget the calm that lies
In disillusioned eyes.
Though we all know that we must die,
Yet you and I
May walk like gods and be
Even now at home in immortality.

We see so many ugly things—
Deceits and wrongs and quarrelings;
We know, alas! we know
How quickly fade
The color in the west,
The bloom upon the flower,
The bloom upon the breast
And youth's blind hour.
Yet keep within your heart
A place apart
Where little dreams may go,
May thrive and grow.
Hold fast—hold fast your dreams!

Louise Driscoll

The Telephone Pad

84

I keep a pad beside the telephone
For messages to all the family.
You see these aimless doodlings on each page?
I find a cryptic message there for me.

Here's John's with all the figures falling down—
A tree, a pole, a vase, a house, a man.
He tries to spare me all his worries, but
I'll help him through again. I know I can.

Our daughter Betty, studious and plain,
Indifferent to boys—what has she meant
By all these broken hearts by arrows pierced?
Tomorrow she shall have a permanent.

These monsters are the work of little Jim.
They're almost scribbled over, but not quite.
He seems so bold and fearless—yet I think
I'll leave a dim light in his room tonight.

I try to pierce the brave mask each one wears.
To catch a soul off guard one needs a sign
That points a way to help and understand.
Oh, yes—those circles and the frames are mine.

Mary Ruth Funk

85

If we would only give, just once,
the same amount of reflection to what
we want to get out of life that we give to the question
of what to do with a two weeks' vacation,
we would be startled at our false standards and
the aimless procession of our busy days.

Dorothy Canfield Fisher

The Task That Is Given to You

86

To each one is given a marble to carve for the wall;
A stone that is needed to heighten the beauty of all;
And only his soul has the magic to give it grace;
And only his hands have the cunning to put it in place.

Yes, the task that is given to each one, no other can do;
So the errand is waiting; it has waited through ages for you.
And now you appear; and the hushed ones are turning their g
To see what you do with your chance in the chamber of days.

Edwin Markham

Time of Life

87

Years, in our youth, are endless;
Years, in old age, are slow.
But the constant riddle
Of years in the middle
Is, where on earth do they go?

Hal Chadwick

88

Do not worry; eat three square meals a day;
say your prayers; be courteous to your creditors;
keep your digestion good; exercise, go slow and easy.
Maybe there are other things your special case requires
to make you happy, but my friend,
these I reckon will give you a good lift.

Abraham Lincoln

89

The only life worth living is the adventurous life. Of such a life the dominant characteristic is that it is unafraid. In the first place, it is unafraid of what other people think. Like Columbus, it dares not only to assert a belief but to live it in the face of contrary opinion. It does not adapt either its pace or its objectives to the pace and objectives of its neighbors. It is not afraid of dreaming dreams that have no practical meaning. It thinks its own thoughts, it reads it own books, it develops its own hobbies, it is governed by its own conscience.

The herd may graze where it pleases or stampede when it pleases, but he who lives the adventurous life will remain unafraid when he finds himself alone.

Raymond B. Fosdick

90

Make no little plans;
they have no magic to stir men's blood
and probably themselves will not be realized.
Make big plans, aim high in hope and work,
remembering that a logical diagram
once recorded will be a living thing
asserting itself with ever-growing insistency.

Daniel H. Burnham

91

It is not he that enters upon any career,
or starts in any race,
but he that runs well and perseveringly,
that gains the plaudits of others
or the approval of his own conscience.

Alexander Campbell

92

Do your work—not just your work and no more,
but a little more for the lavishing's sake;
that little more which is worth all the rest.
And if you suffer as you must,
and if you doubt as you must, do your work.
Put your heart into it and the sky will clear.
Then out of your very doubt and suffering
will be born the supreme joy of life.

Dean Briggs

Hard Lines on a Soft Touch

93

How many a woman has gone
berserk
On being asked with a kindly
smirk,
"Are you a housewife, or do you work?"

Georgie Starbuck Galbraith

Man around the House—Somewhere

94

Where is he when weeds in the garden are sprawling?
He's lolling.
Where is he when leaves on the front lawn are cresting?
He's resting.
Where is he whenever the auto needs hosing?
He's dozing.
And what is the version he gives without blinking?
He's thinking!

Jean Carpenter Mergard

Favorite Performances

95 [One] of my favorite performances took place in Corinth, old Corinth, or what is left of it.

I had been on a motor tour of Greece, careening around that fascinating country with a young couple whom I dearly love... [and], after crossing the Corinthian Canal, we found ourselves in old Corinth. We visited the museum, the Temple of Apollo which had been built some time in the 6th century B.C., the Fountain of Peirene, and the Agora. The Agora, or marketplace, stirred me especially. For, in addition to all the other mental images that this sort of journey into time has a way of creating, I thrilled to the fact that St. Paul had worked and spoken in ancient Corinth. Indeed, it was to his congregation here that he wrote two of his most famous epistles, those two letters that probably contain the best formulation and noblest expression of his ethical values.

Perhaps there was something especially intoxicating in the climate of that sunny day. Perhaps the sun had been a little too strong. But as I walked around I seemed to have jolted myself into the ages and I was terribly moved. When we came to the Rostrum, a little marble slab from which a speaker could look downward to his listeners, our guide explained its use: "Anyone who had something he wished to say could wait his turn, climb on the platform, and harangue the populace." As an afterthought, he let drop "St. Paul is supposed to have spoken from here. Follow me." And he was off to the next site in a great hurry. He was a kind of hint and run liar, that guide. Usually our trio followed behind him, suppressing giggles. But that day I didn't move. I stood gaping at that slab of white marble willing myself to believe that Paul of Tarsus, a man of flesh and blood, had once stood there. The soles of his sandals had pressed on this stone, his voice had sounded in this air. I became possessed of a terrible, an irresistible impulse. Shaking inside, I took a quick look to see that everyone within sight and hearing distance was dark complexioned and looked Greek. I hoped they understood no English, because what I was about to do might have been considered irreverent coming from someone in an old sundress. Assuring myself that I would not be understood by anyone I mounted the Rostrum and called out loud and clear, as to a bustling crowd, the words I had to hear in that place.

Though I speak with the tongues of men and of angels, and have not charity, I am become as sounding brass, or a tinkling cymbal.

And though I have the gift of prophecy, and understand all mysteries, and all knowledge; and though I have all faith, so that I could remove mountains, and have not charity, I am nothing.

And though I bestow all my goods to feed the poor, and though I give my body to be burned, and have not charity, it profiteth me nothing.

Charity suffereth long, and is kind; charity envieth not; charity vaunteth not itself, is not puffed up.

Doth not behave itself unseemly, seeketh not her own, is not easily provoked, thinketh no evil;

Rejoiceth not in iniquity, but rejoiceth in truth;

Beareth all things, believeth all things, hopeth all things, endureth all things.

Charity never faileth: but whether there be prophecies, they shall fail; whether there be tongues, they shall cease; whether there be knowledge, it shall vanish away.

For we know in part, and we prophesy in part.

But when that which is perfect is come, then that which is in part shall be done away.

When I was a child, I spake as a child, I understood as a child, I thought as a child: but when I became a man, I put away childish things.

For now we see through a glass, darkly; but then face to face: now I know in part; but then shall I know even as also I am known.

And now abideth faith, hope, charity, these three; but the greatest of these is charity.

Helen Hayes

96

Ah, but a man's reach should exceed his grasp,
Or what's a heaven for?

Robert Browning

From An Astronaut's Wife...

97

I am a woman of 34 whose life has been conditioned by the world of men and their challenges. I followed my husband through the day-to-day wonder of flight training, through the loneliness of sea duty, until somewhere after my fourth year of marriage I realized with some satisfaction that I had developed into a pretty tough bird! But our reunions reaffirmed my belief that a husband—a man—is a rare, wonderful creature, a pleasure to wait on and love, and that questing man is the finest spirit that flies.

I believe that man was not meant to be tamed exclusively to hearth and home, to pillow and procreation. There are few moments of truth left for him in our digit-ridden, security-conscious society, and a woman must be ready to risk her carefully collected store of crystal to gain that rewarding moment on the beach when the rocket shoots out of the smoke layer, and she can say to herself, "I helped you go!"

Mrs. Scott Carpenter

98

No man is born into the world whose work
Is not born with him; there is always work,
And tools to work withal, for those who will;
And blessed are the horny hands of toil!

James Russell Lowell

99

We have no wings, we cannot soar;
But we have feet to scale and climb
By slow degrees, and more and more,
The cloudy summits of our time.

Henry W. Longfellow

100

Rejoice that man is hurled
From change to change unceasingly,
His soul's wings never furled.

Robert Browning

101

O Lord,
Thou givest us everything,
At the price
Of an effort.

Leonardo Da Vinci

102

There is a tide in the affairs of men,
Which, taken at the flood, leads on to fortune;
Omitted, all the voyage of their life
Is bound in shallows and in miseries.
We must take the current when it serves,
Or lose our ventures.

William Shakespeare

103

The day shall not be up so soon as I
To try the fair adventure of tomorrow.

William Shakespeare

104

Men at some time are masters of their fates:
The fault, dear Brutus, is not in our stars,
But in ourselves, that we are underlings.

William Shakespeare

105

Some men see things as they are
and say, why?
I dream things that never were
and say, why not?

George Bernard Shaw

The Bridge

106

I didn't believe,
Standing on the bank of a river
Which was wide and swift,
That I would cross that bridge
Plaited from thin, fragile reeds
Fastened with bast.
I walked delicately as a butterfly
And heavily as an elephant,
I walked surely as a dancer
And wavered like a blind man.
I didn't believe that I would cross that bridge,
And now that I am standing on the other side,
I don't believe I crossed it.

Leopold Staff

107

The psychologist William Moulton Marston asked 3000 persons: "What have you to live for?"

He was shocked to find that 94 per cent were simply enduring the present while they waited for the future; waited for "something" to happen; waited for children to grow up and leave home; waited for next year; waited for another time to take a long-dreamed-about trip; waited for someone to die; waited for tomorrow without realizing that all anyone ever has is today because yesterday is gone and tomorrow never comes.

Douglas Lurton

108

Never bend your head.
Always hold it high.
Look the world straight in the face.

Helen Keller
To a five-year-old blind child

109

It is seldom that we find out
how great are our resources
until we are thrown upon them.

Christian N. Bovee

110

Life admits not of delays;
when pleasure can be had, it is fit to catch it.
Every hour takes away part of the things that please us,
and perhaps part of our disposition to be pleased.

Samuel Johnson

A Spiritual Heritage

111

In my memory, my grandfather is a patriarchal figure, dressed in black, wearing an underbeard with upper lip shaved clean. When I first knew him he was retired and lived across the alley from our home. He kept a horse and buggy which, on occasion, he shared with us boys. His importance, in my mind then, rested on the beard and the buggy and the horse; not on his success as a farmer, or as a leader of the family migration. Now I know otherwise.

My grandfather was more than fifty years old when he determined to take his family and leave the pleasant valley where he had lived a half century. This was, I would guess, the great adventure of his life—to risk his possessions and his comforts, to go from the home country where his fathers had lived from the time they settled in America, to start a new life on a new kind of ground.

For all his vision, he had no reason to think that a century and a quarter after he himself was born, his grandson would return to the Susquehanna River area, hoping to end his days on a Pennsylvania farm. Just that has come to pass. Little more than a few score miles, even as the roads here wind and dip, separates my barn from my grandfather's, still standing in the Lykens valley. In a sense, and not only geographical, I have returned to the home country my grandparents left.

For him to go took courage. And there is a monument to his memory, on the lawn before the house, his Elizabethville home, just off the highway. It was dedicated while I was President by my brother Milton. My name is in the center of the plaque. This is a compliment I appreciate but I think Jacob Eisenhower's worth rests far more on his deeds, on the family he raised and the spiritual heritage he left them, than on his grandson.

Dwight D. Eisenhower

They That Wait Upon the Lord

112

Hast thou not known?
Hast thou not heard,
that the everlasting God,
the Lord
the Creator of the ends of the earth,
fainteth not,
neither is weary?
there is no searching of his understanding.

He giveth power to the faint,
and to them that have no might
he increaseth strength.

Even the youths shall faint
and be weary,
and the young men shall utterly fall.

But they that wait upon the Lord
shall renew their strength:
they shall mount up with wings as eagles,
they shall run and not be weary,
and they shall walk,
and not faint.

Isaiah 40:28-31

113

Real joy comes not from ease or riches
or from the praise of men,
but from doing something worthwhile.

Wilfred T. Grenfell

114

Ideals are like stars;
you will not succeed in touching them with your hands,
but like the seafaring man on the desert of waters,
you choose them as your guides, and,
following them, you reach your destiny.

Carl Schurz

115

The epitaph for Winston Churchill
is that he transcended his own time and country.
He remains a symbol of the triumphant human spirit,
optimistic, youthful and joyful,
even when God was shaking creation.

James Reston

116

He telleth the number of the stars;
he calleth them all by their names.

Psalm 147:4

117

There they stand, the innumerable stars,
shining in order like a living hymn,
written in light.

Nathaniel Parker Willis

118

David Livingstone, the great explorer and Christian pioneer,
wrote in one magnificent sentence,
"I will go anywhere—provided it be forward."

Walter Russell Bowie

119

I could tell where the lamplighter was
by the trail he left behind him.

Harry Lauder

120

Good manners and soft words have brought
many a difficult thing to pass.

Aesop

Temper Tantrum

121

Faced with this juvenile crisis,
I'm always calm and mature;
As cool as a lemon ice is,
Steady, soft-spoken and sure;
Expression deliberate and mild,
Manner composed and benign;
Provided, of course, that the child
Isn't mine.

Betty Billipp

122

A boy's parents prepared the
usual set of addressed cards
for their son to mail home from camp,
but waited in vain for any to show up in the mail.
An anxious inquiry by telephone got this explanation:
"None of the fellows would take them to the box for me."

Marcelene Cox

It Gives Me Great Pleasure

123 "It gives me great pleasure," says the program chairman, and she and I know that she is, like a croquet player, up to the last two wickets. The audience must know, too, that she is approaching the stake because there have been few introductions on any platform that did not wind up with, "and so it gives me great pleasure to present—" But this is the point at which only the chairman and I, from past experience, share an anxiety. Sometimes I am standing in the wings waiting to hear myself introduced; frequently I am in a chair behind her. Wherever I am, my toes are curled with anxiety, and from the way she shifts her position at this point, I have a conviction that hers are too. Will she accomplish the who I am and what I am?

A club president introducing my friend Helen Howe for a program of monologues, caused that artist some anxiety. Miss Howe is the distinguished daughter of the distinguished Mark Antony DeWolfe Howe. The club president, however, in an erratic carom shot, rendered it: "It gives me great pleasure to introduce the distinguished daughter of the distinguished Mark Antony DeWolfe Hopper, winner himself of the Pulsifer Prize for writing the Barrett Wendell Letters," and then she hit the stake. "Miss Helen Howe," she concluded with a triumphant dip in the direction of the astonished Miss Howe.

A president in Minnesota shot through to me, however, with disconcerting accuracy.

"Ladies," she said, "I know how disappointed all of us were not to have General Romulo with us this afternoon, and so afraid that we would not have a program at all, we would have been glad of anybody. It therefore gives me great pleasure to introduce Miss Emily Kimbrough."

124 The greater the obstacle
the more glory in overcoming it.

Moliere

125 If a man does not keep pace with his companions,
perhaps it is because he hears
the beat of a different drummer.
Let him step to the music which he hears,
however measured or far away.

Henry David Thoreau

126 O strong of heart, go where the road
Of ancient honour climbs.
Bow not your craven shoulders,
Earth conquered gives the stars.

Boethius

127 Hitch your wagon to a star.

Ralph Waldo Emerson

128 Greatly begin! Though thou have time
But for a line, be that sublime—
Not failure, but low aim is crime.

James Russell Lowell

129 As soon as you feel too old
to do a thing, do it.

Margaret Deland

The Sparrow Hawk

130

In the morning, with the change that comes on suddenly in that high country, the mist that had hovered below us in the valley had gone. The sky was a deep blue, and one could see for miles over the high outcroppings of stone. I was up early and brought the box in which the little hawk was imprisoned out onto the grass where I was building a cage. A wind as cool as a mountain spring ran over the grass and stirred my hair. It was a fine day to be alive. I looked up and all around and at the hole in the cabin roof out of which the other little hawk had fled. There was no sign of her anywhere that I could see.

"Probably in the next county by now," I thought cynically, but before beginning work I decided I'd have a look at my last night's capture.

Secretively, I looked again all around the camp and up and down and opened the box. I got him right out in my hand with his wings folded properly and I was careful not to startle him. He lay limp in my grasp and I could feel his heart pound under the feathers but he only looked beyond me and up.

I saw him look that last look away beyond me into a sky so full of light that I could not follow his gaze. The little breeze flowed over me again, and nearby a mountain aspen shook all its tiny leaves. I suppose I must have had an idea then of what I was going to do, but I never let it come up into consciousness. I just reached over and laid the hawk on the grass.

He lay there a long minute without hope, unmoving, his eyes still fixed on that blue vault above him. It must have been that he was already so far away in heart that he never felt the release from my hand. He never even stood. He just lay with his breast against the grass.

In the next second after that long minute he was gone. Like a flicker of light, he had vanished with my eyes full on him, but without actually seeing even a premonitory wing beat. He was gone straight into that towering emptiness of light and crystal that my eyes could scarcely bear to penetrate. For another long moment there was silence. I could not see him. The light was too intense. Then from far up somewhere a cry came ringing down.

I was young then and had seen little of the world, but when I heard that hawk cry my heart turned over. It was not the cry of the hawk I had captured; for, by shifting my position against the sun, I was now seeing further up. Straight out of the sun's eye, where she must have been soaring restlessly above us for untoward hours, hurtled his mate. And from far up, ringing from peak to peak of the summits over us, came a cry of such unutterable and ecstatic joy that it sounds down across the years and tingles among the cups on my quiet breakfast table.

I saw them both now. He was rising fast to meet her. They met in a great soaring gyre that turned into a whirling circle and a dance of wings. Once more, just once, their two voices, joined in a harsh wild medley of question and response, struck and echoed against the pinnacles of the valley. Then they were gone forever somewhere into those upper regions beyond the eyes of men.

Loren Eiseley

131

Though much is taken, much abides; and though
We are not now that strength which in old days
Moved earth and heaven, that which we are, we are,–
One equal temper of heroic hearts,
Made weak by time and fate, but strong in will
To strive, to seek, to find, and not to yield.

Alfred, Lord Tennyson

132

Nothing in the world can take the place of persistence.
Talent will not;
nothing is more common than unsuccessful men with talent.
Genius will not;
unrewarded genius is almost a proverb.
Education will not;
the world is full of educated derelicts.
Persistence and determination alone are omnipotent.
The slogan "press on!" has solved
and always will solve
the problems of the human race.

Calvin Coolidge

133

I find the great thing in this world
is not so much where we stand,
as *in what direction we are moving*.
To reach the port of heaven,
we must sail sometimes with the wind,
and sometimes against it;
but we must sail, and not drift,
nor lie at anchor.

Oliver Wendell Holmes

134

If we are to survive, we must have ideas, vision, courage.
These things are rarely produced by committees.
Everything that matters in our intellectual and moral life
begins with an individual confronting
his own mind and conscience in a room by himself.

Arthur M. Schlesinger, Jr.

135

Let each become all that
He was created capable of being
Expand, if possible, to his full growth
And show himself at length
In his own shape and stature
Be these what they may.

Thomas Carlyle

136

Those having torches
will pass them on to others.

Plato

137

The potential of a child is the
most intriguing thing in all creation.

Ray Lyman Wilbur

138

The winds and waves are always
on the side of the ablest navigators.

Edward Gibbon

139

Yet still there whispers the small voice within,
Heard through God's silence, and o'er glory's din,
Whatever creed be taught, or land be trod,
Man's conscience is the oracle of God.

George Gordon, Lord Byron

Chapter Three

Thank God for Life

Thank God for life; life is not sweet always.
Hands may be heavy laden, heart care-full;
Unwelcome nights follow unwelcome days,
And dreams divine end in awakenings dull;
Still it is life; and life is cause for praise.
This ache, this restlessness, this quickening sting
Prove me no torpid and inanimate thing—
Prove me of Him who is the life, the spring.

I am alive—and that is beautiful.

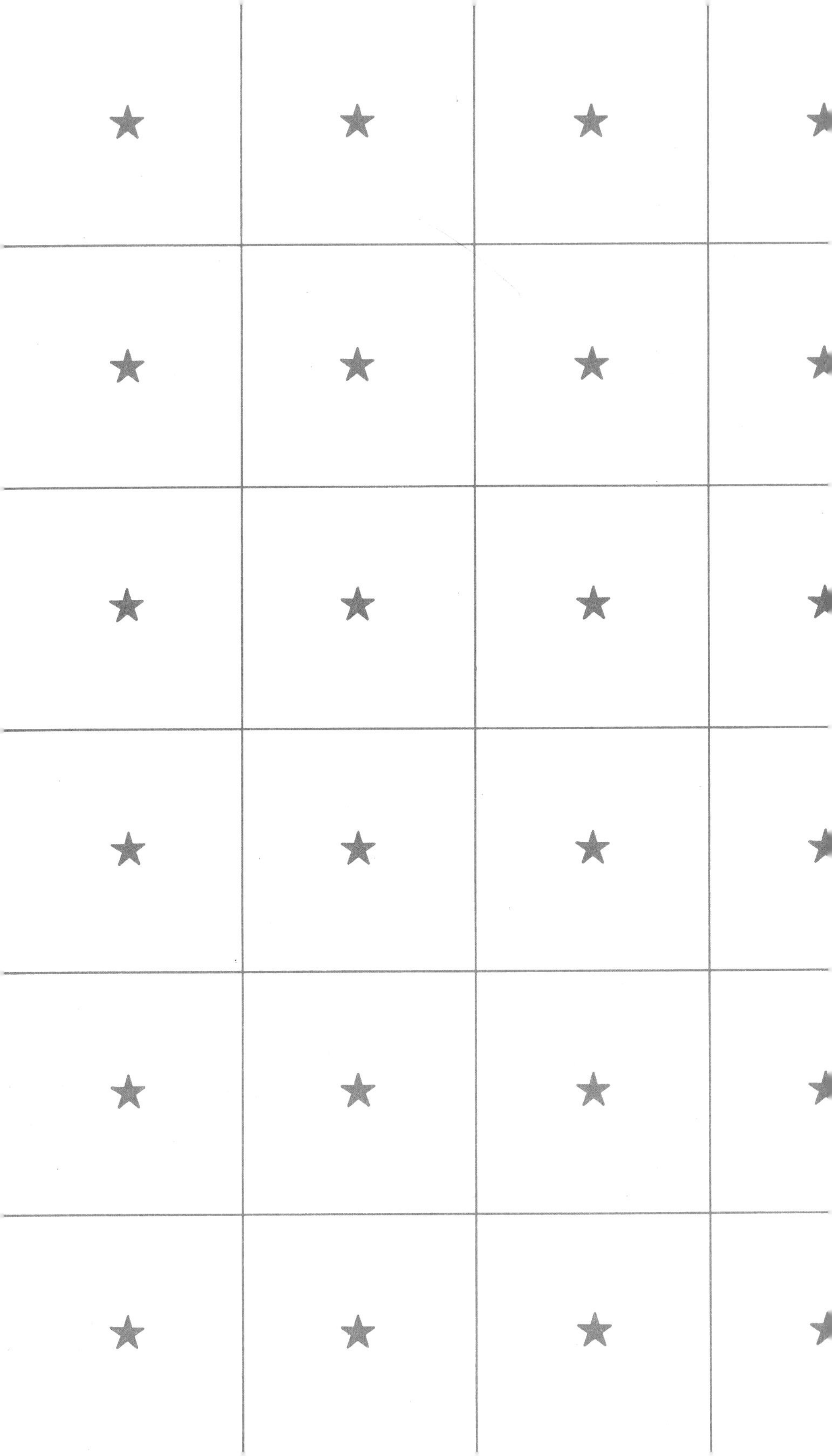

141

If God is on our side, who is against us? He did not spare his own Son, but surrendered him for us all; and with this gift how can he fail to lavish upon us all he has to give? Who will be the accuser of God's chosen ones? It is God who pronounces acquittal: then who can condemn? It is Christ—Christ who died, and more than that, was raised from the dead—who is at God's right hand, and indeed pleads our cause.

Then what can separate us from the love of Christ? Can affliction or hardship? Can persecution, hunger, nakedness, peril, or the sword? 'We are being done to death for thy sake all day long,' as Scripture says; 'we have been treated like sheep for slaughter'—and yet in spite of all, overwhelming victory is ours through him who loved us. For I am convinced that there is nothing in death or life, in the realm of spirits or superhuman powers, in the world as it is or the world as it shall be, in the forces of the universe, in heights or depths—nothing in all creation that can separate us from the love of God in Christ Jesus our Lord.

Romans 8:31-39
New English Bible

Wings

142

Let us be like a bird for a moment perched
On a frail branch while he sings;
Though he feels it bend, yet he sings his song,
Knowing that he has wings.

Victor Hugo

143

Do not stop thinking of life as an adventure.

Eleanor Roosevelt

144

It is the stars
as not known to science that I would know,
the stars which the lonely traveler knows.

Henry David Thoreau

145

If seeds in the black earth
can turn into such beautiful roses,
what might not the heart of man become
in its long journey toward the stars?

Gilbert Keith Chesterton

Watchers of the Sky

146

Newton:
Fools have said
That knowledge drives out wonder from the world;
They'll say it still, though all the dust's ablaze
With miracles at their feet; while Newton's laws
Foretell that knowledge one day shall be song,
And those whom Truth has taken to her heart
Find that it beats in music.

"I know not how my work may seem to others—"
So wrote our mightiest mind—"but to myself
I seem a child that wandering all day long
Upon the sea-shore gathers here a shell,
And there a pebble, colored by the wave,
While the great ocean of truth, from sky to sky
Stretches before him, boundless, unexplored."

Alfred Noyes

147

It is a glorious privilege
to live, to know, to act, to listen, to behold, to love.
To look up at the blue summer sky;
to see the sun sink slowly beyond the line of the horizon;
to watch the worlds come twinkling into view, first one by one,
and the myriads that no man can count,
and lo! the universe is white with them;
and you and I are here.

Marco Morrow

Beyond Doubt

148

The sun, with all those planets moving round it,
can ripen the smallest bunch of grapes
as if it had nothing else to do.
Why then should I doubt His power?

Galileo

Till Faith Move Mountains

149

There is but one way to browbeat this world,
Dumb-founder doubt, and repay scorn in kind,—
To go on trusting, namely, till faith move Mountains.

Robert Browning

150

For we walk by faith, not by sight.

The Apostle Paul
II Corinthians 5:7

151

Life's a pretty precious and wonderful thing.
You can't sit down and let it lap around you...
you have to plunge into it;
you have to dive through it!
And you can't save it, you can't store it up;
you can't hoard it in a vault.
You've got to taste it; you've got to use it.
The more you use, the more you have...
that's the miracle of it!

Kyle Crichton

Daniel and the Weather

152

Daniel liked the open. When it thundered
And other men went in and closed their doors,
Huddled by their stoves and fumed and fretted,
Daniel found imaginary chores
That kept him out from under any roof-top.
He drank a rainstorm, happy as the grass.
There wasn't any kind of day that Daniel
Wanted second-hand through window glass.

He said the way to get along with weather
Was let it soak in deep, clear to the bone.
So if the rain fell in a silver torrent,
Or snowflakes sifted down, or good sun shone,
Daniel would be out in it, going somewhere.
If you asked him in, he'd hold your eye
And tell you, patiently, he'd been appointed
To feel the goodness coming from the sky!

Edna Casler Joll

Thought for Thanksgiving

153

A scarlet tulip nodding in the breeze.
The dewy freshness of an April morn.
  A calf just born.
The endless vastness of the pounding sea.
The quiet peace of snow that falls at night.
  The geese in flight.
The smell of earth fresh-turned beneath the plow.
A misty rainbow arching through the sky.
  A butterfly.
The gentle whisper of cascading leaves.
A gang of puppies romping in the sun.
  The day's work done.

We take Thy blessings, Lord, all through the year
Without a word of thanks until, today,
  We pause to pray.

Barbara Parsons Hildreth

154

When someone questioned Handel
on his feelings when composing
the Hallelujah Chorus of *The Messiah*, he replied:
"I did think I did see all Heaven before me
and the great God Himself."

James Beattie

155

We should act with as much energy
as those who expect everything from themselves;
and we should pray with as much earnestness
as those who expect everything from God.

Charles Caleb Colton

Christmas Wish

156

God give you blessings at Christmas time;
Stars for your darkness, sun for your day,
Light on the path as you search for the Way,
  And a mountain to climb.

God grant you courage this coming year,
Fruit for your striving, friends if you roam,
Joy in your labor, love in your home,
  And a summit to clear.

Myra Scovel

157

Part of me remained forever at Latitude 80° 08′ South:
what survived of my youth,
my vanity, perhaps, and certainly my skepticism.
On the other hand I did take away something
that I had not fully possessed before:
appreciation of the sheer beauty
and miracle of being alive,
and a humble set of values.
All this happened four years ago.
Civilization has not altered my ideas.
I live more simply now, and with more peace.

Admiral Richard E. Byrd

158

To every life there comes a time supreme;
One day, one night, one morning or one noon,
One gladsome hour, one moment opportune,
One rift through which sublime fulfillments gleam.

Grace before Sleep

159

How can our minds and bodies be
Grateful enough that we have spent
Here in this generous room, we three,
This evening of content?
Each one of us has walked through storm
And fled the wolves along the road;
But here the hearth is wide and warm,
And for this shelter and this light
Accept, O Lord, our thanks to-night.

Sara Teasdale

The Borrowers

160

With what presumption have we dared to voice,
"Thank you for home (although we hold the deed),
Our acre, trees, and flowers (ours by choice),
Our faithful dog and cat (though it's agreed
No one can own the latter), each good book
(A gift or purchased), all else we foresaw
That we would cherish, and have made to look
Ours by possession (nine points of the law)."

With what presumption have we called them ours,
And even felt unselfish when we shared them,
When, if the truth be known, they have been Yours
From the beginning, Lord! You have prepared them
For us to borrow, using as our own—
So thank You, rather, for this generous loan.

Elaine V. Emans

161

When the one man loves the one woman
and the one woman loves the one man,
the very angels leave heaven and
come and sit in that house and sing for joy.

Ernest Brahma

Life's Purpose

162

This life were brutish did we not sometimes
Have intimations clear of wider scope,
Hints of occasion infinite, to keep
The soul alert with noble discontent
And onward yearnings of unstilled desire;
Fruitless, except we now and then divined
A mystery of Purpose, gleaming through
The secular confusions of the world,
Whose will we darkly accomplish, doing ours.

James Russell Lowell

163

Perfect happiness, I believe,
was never intended by the Deity to be
the lot of one of His creatures in this world;
but that He has very much put in our power
the nearness of our approaches to it,
is what I have steadfastly believed.

Thomas Jefferson

A Home for Johnny

164

The happiness that Johnny gives me whenever he enters the room, or whenever I look at his picture, is that of a deep content, the sort of feeling one has when a story rightly has a happy ending. For Johnny has a family—who loves him and appreciates him, and it is I who helped him to find his family.

It might have been different. I had to take a chance. Was it right or wrong to tell those young Chinese parents one summer day, so long ago, that they could give me their little son? At first, I could not believe them. How could a father and mother want to give away a beautiful little boy only two years old? They explained it in the letter.

"We have two children," the letter said. "The elder is our first-born son, aged two. The baby is only six months old. We would like to give you our elder son so that he may be brought up in a free country, in the traditions of liberty as we have observed them while we have studied here in the U.S."

The letter came from a distant state and a great university. These parents were not ordinary young people. The letter was intelligent and well-expressed. I could feel deep emotion behind it; but there was also resolution and restraint. The letter proceeded to give me their background. They came from a part of China that I knew very well, and from an ancient city. The father's family was, or had been, well-to-do, not the sudden riches of the opportunist but the wealth of land ownership and an aristocracy of education and breeding. The mother's family was equally good.

"We have been here in the United States for three years studying," the father wrote, "I in English literature and my wife in psychology. We were married in China before coming here, and our family supported us. Now, however, funds have been cut off, and we hear through Hong Kong friends that our family is suffering. Our parents are old, and we have the duty to suffer with them, even if we cannot help. Our son, however..."

The son is Johnny. He was two years old then and, as the letter went on to say, a child of high intelligence and much promise.

"Our families," the young father continued, "have been scholars and intellectuals for thousands of years. Our son, therefore, has an inheritance. We do not wish to see this heritage given over to an ideology which will waste it. If we were to take him back to China with us, he would be put into a state-owned kindergarten at the age of three. He may even at that age be taken from us altogether and put into a state-owned nursery, where he will be beyond our reach. He will no longer be ours. His brother is still a baby and cannot be separated from his mother, but we feel that our son will be able to endure the separation. We give him to you. Please find suitable parents for him, but keep him near you..."

My first impulse was total rejection of the whole idea. Parents give up a child? I wrote back saying that I could not possibly receive such a gift and that the child must stay with his parents. Their love for him was obvious and strong enough to keep him with them, wherever he was.

The reply came quickly. If I would not receive him, the father said, then they would leave him in an American orphanage. The decision was irrevocable, though not easily or quickly made.

I was astounded by their determination. Then I remembered that the letters had all been signed by the father. Perhaps, in her heart, the mother did not agree or at least was reluctant. I waited until I thought the father would be away from home, and then put in a long-distance call. The mother answered the telephone. I knew by the sound of her voice that it was she—a voice soft and cultivated, tender and shy.

"I am calling you about your little boy," I said when I had introduced myself. "Let us talk as woman to woman. Can it be true that you want to give him away?"

"Not just give him away," she replied. "We give him to *you*."

"I appreciate the difference," I told her, "but I cannot bear to take a child from his mother. If I did this, I should think of you as long as I lived. Can I help you in some way? Why go back to China? Stay here in the United States and keep him with you."

The soft voice was clear and firm. "Thank you, but we cannot. We have thought about everything, and it is our duty to return to our home country, first to our old parents and also to do what we can as Chinese. We are not Communists. We do not want our son to be a Communist. We want him to be free. If some day he wishes to be a Communist, he must decide it for himself."

"If you are sure..." I began uncertainly.

"We have decided," she said. "Thank you... and..." Here her voice broke but only for one second. "And, please—love him."

She hung up the receiver before I could promise my love, but I went back to my desk and wrote a short letter to the father: "Bring him to me whenever you wish."

His answer came by wire. "Next Thursday."

Thursday afternoon, I remember, was a warm and beautiful day. The children had gone to the woods to look for wild flowers, and I was alone in the house. I had cut an armful of roses and was arranging them in my silver bowl when the bell rang. The door was open, and I saw them standing there, a slender gentle-looking young Chinese man in Western clothes and a little boy in a new blue suit with a wide, white sailor collar.

"Here you are," I said. "I have been expecting you. And this is Johnny."

"I have told him you are his grandmother," the young man said. "I have told him you will find him a kind American father and mother."

"Come in," I said.

There are moments, sometimes, when we are so near the heart of life itself that reality is too deep. I knew what the father was feeling, and he knew that I knew. I saw such agony in his controlled face that I could only respond with an equal control, lest both of us be lost.

We sat down. One of the puppies came to the door, and the little boy laughed and ran to pick it up. It gave me a chance to make a final appeal.

"Are you sure you must do this?"

"We have considered everything," he said. "Apart from our duty to our parents, there is also the matter of our livelihood. I came here to train myself in English literature, and I hoped to return to my country as a professor. I cannot earn my living here, for no college or school wants a Chinese professor of English literature. I cannot be a waiter or a dishwasher in a restaurant. Then, too, we have a duty to our country, whatever the government is. We have something to give to our people—a knowledge of another way of life."

He clenched his teeth. He would not allow himself tears. "Please—don't try to persuade me."

"You must do what you think is right," I agreed.

He rose abruptly then. "Will you take him for a little walk while I..."

"Yes," I said.

We clasped hands for a moment, and then I went to the little boy. "Let's take the puppy down to the pond and see the goldfish."

He took my hand at once, and we walked out into the sunshine to the pond under the willow trees. We sat on the low stone wall there and watched the fish. After a half hour or so, he was uneasy, and we went back to the house. It was empty.

The young father was gone. I have not seen him since, or ever heard of him or of the young mother. They went back to China, I am sure, and I shall never know, I suppose, what became of them. But I can never forget that moment when the little boy knew his father was not waiting for him. It cut its way deep into my heart and my memory. The child was so beautifully intelligent, so quick to understand what had happened. Perhaps his parents had explained to him. But he gave one great racking sob and turned to me and was silent.

I wrapped him in my arms and held him, the tears running down my cheeks—as they do even now when I remember. How could I ever make it up to him? History with all the sorrow and foolishness of the human race laid its heavy burden on the little boy that day and made him an orphan. What a task to find new parents worthy of him, who would understand him and what he was compelled to suffer!

Yet that was a moment, too, of inspiration. It is not only joy that inspires—sometimes it is grief. I resolved that, with every aid I could summon, I would find the parents who deserved this child. I wished that my husband and I were young enough to keep him, but we were not. He must have young parents who could see him through the years ahead. I devoted myself to the task.

Life has a way of providing its own answers. Before long, I found the two I was looking for, a young couple, talented and warm of heart. They live in a comfortable stone house in the country not too far from me. The father is a scientist, the mother is an artist. There is the idealism of the artist in every true scientist, and the dedication of the scientist in the artist. Johnny has both in him. I knew that the search was ended. We made acquaintance, they and we. Love came spontaneously and without undue delay, and Johnny went to his American home and parents.

I watched him walk away between them on the last day, his hand in theirs, and that, too, was a moment of inspiration. Yes, they were his and he was theirs. My certainty is renewed every time I see Johnny with them, and seven years have passed. He is fulfilling the faith of his Chinese parents in him, too. He is what they told me he was, and his inheritance of generations of fine Chinese men and women is finding its full development here in a new country. He will be a great Chinese and a great American.

Pearl S. Buck

165

Die when I may,
I want it said of me by those who knew me best,
that I always plucked a thistle and planted a flower
where I thought a flower should grow.

Abraham Lincoln

166

Pleasure is seldom found where it is sought.
Our brightest blazes are
commonly kindled by unexpected sparks.

Samuel Johnson

167

God gave man an upright countenance
to survey the heavens,
and to look upward to the stars.

Ovid

The Simple Things

168

Give me the simple things close to my home
The things that are familiar, old and dear,
I do not have to wander far, or roam
The Seven Seas—when I have splendor here.

Give me a crackling flame upon the grate
And the warm smell of bread upon the fire.
I do not have to ride abroad in state
To find the very core of heart's desire.

A shining tea-pot—friendly hands to pour
And jam that smells of grapes from our own vine.
Could any noble king desire more?
I am a king myself, for these are mine.

Let those who will seek promised lands afar,
For treasures so remote I shed no tears.
Why should I strive to reach a distant star
When heaven with all its beauty is right here!

Lines Written in Her Breviary

169

Let nothing disturb thee,
Nothing affright thee;
All things are passing:
God never changeth;
Patient endurance
Attaineth to all things;
Who God possesseth
In nothing is wanting;
Alone God sufficeth.

St. Theresa
(translated by Henry Wadsworth Longfellow)

170

A religion that is
small enough for our understanding
would not be large enough for our needs.

Arthur Balfour

171

The longer I live
the more my mind dwells upon the
beauty and the wonder of the world.
I hardly know which feeling leads,
wonderment or admiration.

John Burroughs

Silence

172

I need not shout my faith. Thrice eloquent
Are quiet trees and the green listening sod;
Hushed are the stars, whose power is never spent;
The hills are mute: yet how they speak of God!

Charles Hanson Towne

173

A handful of pine-seed will cover mountains
with the green majesty of forest.
I too will set my face to the wind
and throw my handful of seed on high.

Fiona Macleod

174

There's a divinity that shapes our ends,
Rough-hew them how we will.

William Shakespeare

Green Words Will Rise

175

I saw him at the summer side of autumn,
Striding the lip of field against the sky.
His arm wrote out the lovely, flowing sentence,
Dipped from the sling of seed against his thigh.

This was the way he liked to sow his clover,
While neighbors worked with tractor and with drill;
As men do, when they look on something holy,
I trembled—and the day stood very still.

For here were hand, and seed, and earth together,
Writing the script for all our witnessing;
New type will rise beneath the hands of sowers,
And I'll read green words on the page of spring.

Ralph W. Seager

176

At the heart of the life of Albert Schweitzer
there is the feeling of indebtedness to Almighty God.
"I was stabbed awake one morning with the realization
that I could not accept life's happiness
as a matter of course," he has written.
"I must give something in return.
I was made to see the deeper meaning of the passage
'He that loseth his life shall find it.'"
He gathered up his life philosophy
in four unforgettable sentences:

"To know the will of God is the greatest knowledge.
To suffer the will of God is the greatest heroism.
To do the will of God is the greatest achievement.
To have the approval of God on your work is
the greatest happiness."

Frank A. Court

177

Jesus said, I am the resurrection and the life:
he that believeth in me,
though he were dead, yet shall he live:
And whosoever liveth and believeth in
me shall never die.

John 11:25, 26

178

Bad will be the day for every man when he
becomes absolutely contented with the life that he is living,
with the thoughts that he is thinking,
with the deeds that he is doing,
when there is not forever beating at the doors of his soul
some great desire to do something larger,
which he knows that he was meant and made to do
because he is still, in spite of all, the child of God.

Phillips Brooks

179

Nor love thy life, nor hate; but whilst thou liv'st
Live well; how long, how short, permit to Heaven.

John Milton

180

Every year I live I am more convinced
that the waste of life
lies in the love we have not given,
the powers we have not used,
the selfish prudence that will risk nothing,
and which, shirking pain, misses happiness as well.
No one ever yet was the poorer in the long run
for having once in a lifetime
"let out all the length of all the reins."

Mary Cholmondeley

181

Dare to be wise; begin!
He who postpones the hour of living rightly
is like the rustic who waits for the river
to run out before he crosses.

Horace

182

Begin at once to live,
and count each day
as a separate life.

Seneca

Stars

183

Ye stars! which are the poetry of heaven,
If in your bright leaves we would read the fate
Of men and empires—'t is to be forgiven
That in our aspirations to be great
Our destinies o'erleap their mortal state,
And claim a kindred with you; for ye are
A beauty and a mystery, and create
In us such love and reverence from afar,
That fortune, fame, power, life, have named
themselves a star.

George Gordon, Lord Byron

184

Man is his own star; and the soul that can
Render an honest and a perfect man,
Commands all light, all influence, all fate;
Nothing to him falls early or too late.

Francis Beaumont and John Fletcher

Miracle

185

Do not pray for easy lives;
pray to be stronger men.
Do not pray for tasks equal to your powers;
pray for powers equal to your tasks.
Then the doing of your work shall be no miracle,
but you shall be a miracle.
Every day you shall wonder at yourself,
at the richness of life
which has come to you by the grace of God.

Phillips Brooks

186

It takes solitude, under the stars,
for us to be reminded of
our eternal origin and our far destiny.

Archibald Rutledge

Acknowledgments

The author-compiler and the publisher have made every effort to trace the ownership of all copyrighted material and to secure permission from holders of such material. In the case of inadvertent omission, the author-compiler and the publisher will be pleased to make the necessary corrections in future printings. Thanks are due to the following authors, publishers, publications and agents for permission to use the material indicated:

Margaret T. Applegarth and Harper & Row, Publishers, Inc. for a specified selection from *Men As Trees Walking* by Margaret T. Applegarth, Copyright © 1952 by Harper & Row, Publishers, Inc.

Richard Armour for permission to reprint the poem, *It Could Be Worse* by Richard Armour.

Russell Baker and *The New York Times* for *Observer: Don't Make the Kids Do It All* by Russell Baker which appeared in *The New York Times*, September 12, 1965, Copyright © 1965 by The New York Times Company.

Betty Billipp and *McCall's* magazine for *Temper Tantrum* by Betty Billipp. Reprinted by permission from the October, 1967 issue of *McCall's* magazine, Copyright © 1967 by The McCall Corporation.

John Mason Brown and Whittlesey House, McGraw-Hill Book Company, Inc. for two specified selections from *Morning Faces* by John Mason Brown, Copyright © 1949 by John Mason Brown and published by Whittlesey House, McGraw-Hill Book Company, Inc. Reprinted by permission of John Mason Brown.

Pearl S. Buck and Harold Ober Associates Incorporated for *A Home for Johnny (My Most Inspiring Moment)* by Pearl S. Buck, which appeared in *Family Weekly*, July 16, 1961, Copyright © 1961 by Pearl S. Buck. Reprinted by permission of Harold Ober Associates Incorporated.

Cambridge University Press for permission to use Romans 8:31–39 from *The New English Bible, New Testament* © The Delegates of the Oxford University Press and The Syndics of the Cambridge University Press 1961.

Anne Campbell and Doubleday & Company, Inc. for *To Give A Child A Dream* by Anne Campbell. Reprinted by permission of Anne Campbell.

Ruth and Hal Chadwick and The Methodist Publishing House for *There's Something Nice About Having Them Around* by Ruth and Hal Chadwick. From *Together* magazine, November 1965, Copyright © 1965 by The Methodist Publishing House.

Hal Chadwick and The Methodist Publishing House for *Time of Life* by Hal Chadwick. From *Together* magazine, January 1959, Copyright © by Lovick Pierce. Reprinted by permission of The Methodist Publishing House.

Mary C. Crichton and Berle and Berle for permission to reprint a specified selection from *The Happiest Millionaire*, Copyright © 1967 by Kyle Crichton (Original Title: *My Philadelphia Father by* Cordelia Drexel Biddle as told to Kyle Crichton, Copyright © 1955 by Kyle Crichton, Copyright © 1955 by The McCall Corporation.) Reprinted by permission of Mrs. Kyle Crichton.

Marie Dane and *McCall's* magazine for *Sheltered Wife* by Marie Dane. Reprinted by permission from the March, 1968 issue of *McCall's* magazine, Copyright © 1968 by The McCall Corporation.

Barbara Shook Conklin and The Curtis Publishing Company for *Lucinda* by Barbara Shook Conklin. Reprinted with premission from *Ladies' Home Journal*, Copyright © 1956, The Curtis Publishing Company.

Marcelene Cox and The Curtis Publishing Company for one specified selection from each of the following *Ask Any Woman* columns by Marcelene Cox: May, 1956; July, 1956; October 1956; and December, 1958. Reprinted with permission from *Ladies' Home Journal*, Copyright © 1956 and Copyright © 1958, The Curtis Publishing Company.

Harold Dunn and *Today's Education* for *Christmas Grows on Many Trees* by Harold Dunn, teacher, Ballwin and Westridge Elementary Schools, Ballwin, Missouri. Reprinted by permission of Harold Dunn and *Today's Education*.

Will Durant and *Pace* magazine for a specified selection from *Man Is Wiser Than Any Man* which appeared in *The Reader's Digest*, November, 1968, Copyright © 1968 by Pace Publications, Moral Re-Armament, Inc. Reprinted by permission of *Pace* magazine.

General Dwight D. Eisenhower and Doubleday & Company, Inc. for a specified selection from *At Ease* by Dwight D. Eisenhower, Copyright © 1967 by Dwight D. Eisenhower.

Loren Eisley and Random House, Inc. for a specified selection from *The Immense Journey* by Loren Eiseley, Copyright © 1955 by Loren Eiseley.

Elaine V. Emans and *McCall's* magazine for *The Borrowers by Elaine* V. Emans. Reprinted by permission from the November, 1962 issue of *McCall's* magazine, Copyright © 1962 by The McCall Corporation.

Raymond B. Fosdick for permission to reprint a specified selection from an address made to the graduating class at Smith College, Northampton, Massachusetts, in 1929.

Mary Ruth Funk and The Curtis Publishing Company for *The Telephone Pad* by Mary Ruth Funk. Reprinted with permission from *Ladies' Home Journal*, Copyright © 1956, The Curtis Publishing Company.

Georgie Starbuck Galbraith and The Curtis Publishing Company for *Seventeen, Hard Lines On a Soft Touch* and *Marginal Note On a Milk Bill* by Georgie Starbuck Galbraith. Reprinted by permission from *Ladies' Home Journal*, Copyright © 1956, 1958, and 1958 respectively; and by permission of the author, Georgie Starbuck Galbraith.

Elsie Gibbs and The Curtis Publishing Company for *Four* by Elsie Gibbs. Reprinted with permission from *The Saturday Evening Post*, Copyright © 1955 The Curtis Publishing Company.

Jane Goodsell and Doubleday & Company, Inc. for *Nobody Knows the Quandries I've Seen* and *Forty Is Forty* from *I've Only Got Two Hands and I'm Busy Wringing Them* by Jane Goodsell, Copyright © 1960, 1961, 1962, 1963, 1964, 1965, 1966 by Jane Goodsell.

Mildred R. Grenier and The Methodist Publishing House for *Walking With Grandma* by Mildred R. Grenier. From *Together* magazine, April, 1959, Copyright © 1959 by Lovick Pierce.

Mrs. Arthur Guiterman for permission to reprint a specified selection from *Hills* by Arthur Guiterman.

J. B. Handelsman and The Saturday Review, Inc. for a specified cartoon caption which appeared in the *Saturday Review*, June 3, 1967, Copyright © 1967, Saturday Review, Inc.

Harcourt, Brace & World, Inc. for a specified selection from *Affectionately, F.D.R.* Copyright © 1959 by James Roosevelt and Sidney Shalett.

Helen Hayes and M. Evans and Company, Inc. for two specified selections from *A Gift of Joy* by Helen Hayes and Lewis Funke, Copyright © 1965 by Helen Hayes and Lewis Funke. Reprinted by permission of M. Evans and Company, Inc.

Claribel C. Heinen and The Methodist Publishing House for a specified selection from *The Wicked Flea*, Copyright © 1960 by The Methodist Publishing House. Reprinted from the June, 1960, issue of *Together* magazine, by permission of the publisher.

Janet Henry and The Curtis Publishing Company for *Dining Out, Lines to Four Small Children*, and *Necessary Evil*, all by Janet Henry. Reprinted by permission from *Ladies' Home Journal*, Copyright © 1958 The Curtis Publishing Company.

Barbara Parsons Hildreth and *McCall's* magazine for *Thought for Thanksgiving* by Barbara Parsons Hildreth. Reprinted by permission from the November 1963 issue of *McCall's* magazine, Copyright © 1963 by The McCall Corporation.

Elizabeth Starr Hill, *The Reader's Digest*, and Brandt & Brandt for a specified selection from *The Young Girl's Gift* by Elizabeth Starr Hill, Copyright © 1966 by The Reader's Digest Association, Inc. Reprinted by permission of Brandt & Brandt.

Marjorie Holmes and Doubleday & Company, Inc. for *Dad, I Need Some Money*, Copyright © 1963 by The McCall Corporation; *Mother's Day* and *Father's Day;* all from *Love and Laughter* by Marjorie Holmes, Copyright © 1967 Doubleday & Company, Inc.

Holt, Rinehart and Winston, Inc. for permission to reprint a specified selection from *The Squirrel Cage* by Dorothy Canfield Fisher, Copyright © 1912 by Henry Holt & Company.

Kenneth Joll for *David and the Weather* from *The Plumcot Tree* by Edna Casler Joll, Copyright © 1965 by Kenneth Joll, Boise, Idaho.

Jean Kerr and Doubleday & Company, Inc. for *Etiquette for Children* by Jean Kerr, Copyright © 1959 by The Curtis Publishing Company. From the book, *The Snake Has All the Lines* by Jean Kerr.

Emily Kimbrough and Harper & Row, Publishers, Inc. for a specified selection from *It Gives Me Great Pleasure* by Emily Kimbrough which originally appeared in *The New Yorker* magazine, Copyright © 1948 by Emily Kimbrough.

Alfred A. Knopf, Inc. for permission to reprint ten lines from *On Children* by Kahlil Gibran. Reprinted from *The Prophet* by Kahlil Gibran, by permission of the publisher, Alfred A. Knopf, Inc., Copyright © 1923 by Kahlil Gibran; renewal copyright © 1951 by Administrators C.T.A. of Kahlil Gibran Estate, and Mary G. Gibran.

Sibyl Krausz and The Curtis Publishing Company for *Evening Song* by Sibyl Krausz. Reprinted with permission from *Ladies' Home Journal,* Copyright © 1958, The Curtis Publishing Company.

Madeleine Laeufer and The Methodist Publishing House for *Poor Grandma* by Madeleine Laeufer. From *Together* magazine, January, 1967, Copyright © 1967 by The Methodist Publishing House.

John Kord Lagemann, *Christian Herald,* and *The Reader's Digest* for permission to reprint a specified selection from *Bring to It the Rainbow* by John Kord Lagemann which appeared in *Christian Herald,* November, 1966, and *The Reader's Digest,* November, 1966. Reprinted by permission of *The Reader's Digest.*

Mary Wright Lamb and The Curtis Publishing Company for *Asleep* by Mary Wright Lamb. Reprinted with permission from *Ladies' Home Journal,* Copyright © 1956, The Curtis Publishing Company.

Bernard Lansky and The Chicago Tribune-New York News Syndicate, Inc. for a specified selection by Bernard Lansky. Reprinted by permission of the Chicago Tribune-New York News Syndicate.

J. B. Lippincott Company for permission to reprint a specified selection from *Mince Pie* by Christopher Morley, Copyright © 1919, 1947 by Christopher Morley, J. B. Lippincott Company, Publishers.

J. B. Lippincott Company for permission to reprint fourteen lines from *Newton, VIII* in *Part 1: Watchers of the Sky* of *The Torch-Bearers* from *Collected Poems* by Alfred Noyes, Copyright, © 1906, 1934 by Alfred Noyes.

Douglas Ellsworth Lurton and McGraw-Hill Book Company for a specified selection from *The Power of Positive Living* by Douglas Ellsworth Lurton, Copyright © 1950 by McGraw-Hill Book Company.

Sylvia R. Lyons and *McCall's* magazine for *A Mother's Prayer* by Sylvia R. Lyons. Reprinted by permission from the February, 1960 issue of *McCall's* magazine, Copyright © 1960 by The McCall Corporation.

The Macmillan Company for permission to reprint *Grace Before Sleep* from *Collected Poems* by Sara Teasdale, Copyright © 1933 by The Macmillan Company.

Virgil Markham for permission to reprint *Earth Is Enough* and *The Task That Is Given To You* by Edwin Markham.

Jane Merchant and The Methodist Publishing House for *The Seeker* by Jane Merchant, from *Together* magazine, December 1959, Copyright © 1959 by Lovick Pierce; and for *For A Bride and Groom* by Jane Merchant, from *Together* magazine, January 1960, and *Petals of Light* by Jane Merchant, poems copyright © 1960 by Lovick Pierce (Abingdon Press).

Jean Carpenter Mergard and The Methodist Publishing House for three poems which appeared in *Together* magazine: *Unexceptional Behavior*, July 1966, Copyright © 1966; *The Secret*, May 1965, Copyright © 1965; and *Man Around the House–Somewhere*, August 1967, Copyright © 1967, all by The Methodist Publishing House.

Floyd Miller and the *Reader's Digest* for *The Expectant Grandfather's Guidebook* by Floyd Miller. Reprinted by permission of Floyd Miller from the April 1968 *Reader's Digest*, Copyright © 1968 by The Reader's Digest Association, Inc. Condensed from *Harvest Years.*

Joseph F. Morris and *Good Housekeeping* magazine for *Classroom Classics* by Joseph F. Morris. Reprinted from the January, 1968 issue of *Good Housekeeping* magazine, Copyright © 1968 by the Hearst Corporation, by permission of Joseph F. Morris and *Good Housekeeping* magazine.

Bonaro W. Overstreet and W. W. Norton & Company, Inc. for *Assurance*, from *Hands Laid Upon the Wind* by Bonaro W. Overstreet, Copyright © 1955 by W. W. Norton & Company, Inc.

G. P. Putnam's Sons for permission to reprint a specified selection from *Alone* by Admiral Richard E. Byrd, Copyright © 1938 G. P. Putnam's Sons, Inc.

James Reston and *The New York Times* for a specified selection from the James Reston article which appeared on the editorial page of *The New York Times*, February 16, 1965, Copyright © 1965 by The New York Times Company. Reprinted by permission of *The New York Times.*

Arthur M. Schlesinger, Jr. and The Curtis Publishing Company for a specified selection from *The Decline of Greatness* which appeared in *The Saturday Evening Post*, November 1, 1958, Copyright © 1958 by The Curtis Publishing Company. Reprinted by permission of Arthur M. Schlesinger, Jr. and The Curtis Publishing Company.

Myra Scovel for *Christmas Wish* from *Such Bounty* by Myra Scovel.

Charles Scribner's Sons for permission to reprint a specified selection from *On Being Alive* by Walter Russell Bowie, Copyright © 1931 by Charles Scribner's Sons; and for permission to reprint from the writings of Henry van Dyke.

Ralph W. Seager and The Methodist Publishing House for *Familiar Stranger* from *Together* magazine, May 1965, Copyright © 1965, and *Green Words Will Rise* from *Together* magazine, September 1966, Copyright © 1966 by The Methodist Publishing House.

Beulah Fenderson Smith and The Methodist Publishing House for *Hey, Mom!* by Beulah Fenderson Smith. From *Together* magazine, June 1965, Copyright © 1965 by The Methodist Publishing House.

Leopold Staff and Doubleday & Company, Inc. for *The Bridge* by Leopold Staff, from *Postwar Polish Poetry* selected and translated by Czeslaw Milosz, Copyright © 1965 by Czeslaw Milosz.

Loydean Thomas and *McCall's* magazine for a specified selection from *Love Is Not a Trip to the Stars* by Loydean Thomas. Reprinted by permission of Loydean Thomas from the September 1967 issue of *McCall's* magazine, Copyright © 1967 by The McCall Corporation.

Irma Blackford Tierney and *McCall's* magazine for *Compensation* by Irma Blackford Tierney. Reprinted by permission from the October, 1967 issue of *McCall's* magazine, Copyright © 1967 by The McCall Corporation.

Ralphe M. White and The Curtis Publishing Company for a specified selection from *Queen Mother Elizabeth–The World's Most Famous Grandmother* by Ralphe M. White, as told to Heather Graham Fisher. Reprinted with permission from *Ladies' Home Journal*, Copyright © 1961, The Curtis Publishing Company.

Elizabeth Yates for *Jimmy and His Cowboy Belt*, an extract from an address by Elizabeth Yates delivered before the International Writers' Conference, Green Lake, Wisconsin, July, 1961.